About The Collector

Jim Cooley was born a collector. A native to San Diego, he began his love for collecting some eighty years ago. Not able to recall the first item purchased in his collection, he is quite certain it was either a car or a toy train. In fact, Jim proudly displays the first electric train he was given by his parents, a brand new 1938 American Flyer in his bedroom. This will likely be covered in a future volume of Cooley's Collection literature. His 1930 Ford Model A (see page 62) has not been with him as long as his American Flyer, but it comes in a close second. The Model A is the first car Cooley added to his Automobile Collection and is still in his collection today. At the time of purchase, he did not know that he was starting his car collection. He was merely buying a reliable source of transportation for $50. In recent years, with the support of his wife, Carmen Cooley, the two have grown the collection into one of the finest antique automobile collections out there.

In the following pages, we will focus specifically on the hand picked automobiles Jim has chosen to be part of his collection. It is said that the antique automobile collection of the J.A. Cooley Museum is one of the most extensive collection of 100 year old vehicles in the world. The information discussed within is not meant as a factual reference guide, but rather is merely Jim Cooley's recollection of the development of the automobile industry. With the help of some photography provided by Roger Maioroff, we are able to retell Jim's story through each piece of his collection.

Table of Contents

The Automobile Collection at the J. A. Cooley Museum specifically focuses on telling the story behind the evolution of the automobile. For this reason, we find it most appropriate to start this story from the beginning, with the horse drawn carriage. There are two carriages currently in the Cooley Collection. The earlier of the two is displayed in the photograph below. This carriage boasts a metal plate on it's rear axle designating the builder as E. A. Gardner. It still has its original body and wheels. This item is the only lightweight horse buggy that was built in San Diego that is known to exist today! It was purchased new in 1895 by a local couple. In over 120 years, this carriage has had only three owners! In the early 1970s, Jim Cooley

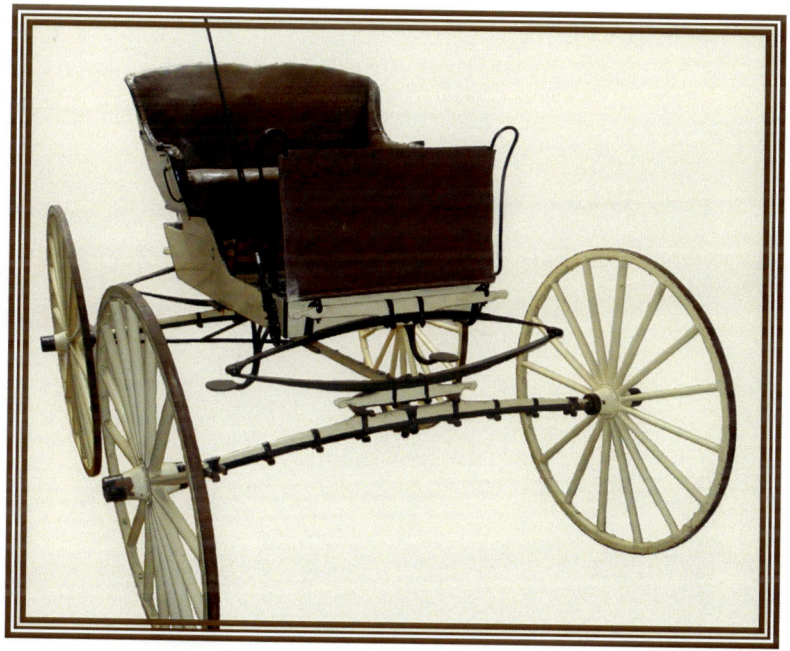

purchased it in Alpine, California from the daughter of the original owners.

To the left is a photograph of the other carriage in the Cooley Collection. It is a 1900 Doctor's Buggy. As noted by it's name, the Doctor's Buggies were geared for doctors' use. Specifically, they were designed for one person because with a lighter load faster speeds could be obtained. While it may be difficult to note in these photographs, a common feature of horse drawn carriages is that the rear wheels are several inches larger than the front ones. This allows for easier turning ability in the front and more braking surface on the rear tires. Another common feature amongst all carriages before the turn of the century is that their tires are all metal. Blacksmiths would ensure a tight fit on the wooden spokes by setting the metal tire onto the rim with extreme heat. This technique is called shrinking the tire.

Horse drawn carriages, such as these, were reliable sources of transportation for hundreds of years. However, they did come with their setbacks. For starters, there was the cost for care of a horse. Additionally, it took longer to prepare the horse and carriage for the travels, and during travel, fatigue would often set in, making it impossible to sustain higher speeds for long periods of time. These setbacks sparked a movement that began in Germany to find other sources of transportation.

1885 Benz Model 1

People were challenged with the task of finding a self-powered form of transportation and they were experimenting with multiple forms, including electric, gas, and steam powered engines. Ultimately, Karl Benz, the

founder of Mercedes-Benz, was the first to respond to this challenge. He is credited with the creation of the world's first automobile, the 1885 Benz Model 1, because it is the first vehicle to offer an internal combustion engine. The Benz Model 1, also known as the Benz Patent Motorwagen, is a three-wheeler with a single speed transmission with one forward gear, and a single cylinder 3/4 horsepower engine. The Model 1 also features rack and pinion steering and a flat belt drive. The engine is connected to the wheels with a flat belt to a jack shaft, and a chain drive to the rear wheels. There is a clutch operated by foot pedal. The car uses benzene that passes through a long narrow manifold to the cylinder. Benzene is used instead of gasoline because it is a much

more volatile fuel that vaporizes more efficiently than gasoline. The braking system for this vehicle consists of a block rubbing against the wheel, similar to the braking technology in horse drawn carriages.

In 1888, Karl's wife, Bertha Benz, used his invention to travel from Mannheim to Pforzheim (approximately 70 miles) to visit her mother. Her travels marked the world's first long distance road trip, which is still celebrated in Germany today with the Bertha Benz Memorial Route.

In the mid-thirties, the Mercedes Benz Company discovered documents containing the original patent drawings by Karl Benz. The company offered a contest in which participants would be given a set of plans for the Model 1 from which they could rebuild the car. The winner of the contest would be awarded $1,000. To our knowledge, these are the earliest models that are still in existence today.

Karl Benz followed his success of the Benz Model 1 with the production of several different car models, one of which being the Benz Velo. The Benz Velo is the world's first mass produced vehicle. It was produced from 1894 through 1901. In 1894, sixty-

1895 Benz Velo

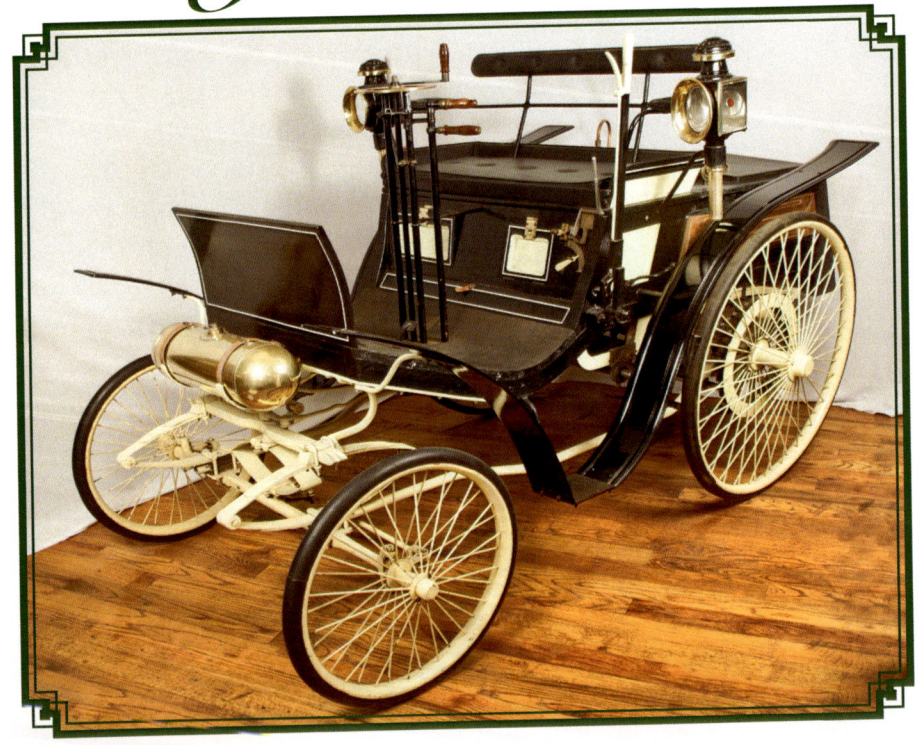

seven were built. This increased to one hundred and thirty-four in 1895. These models were not produced by Karl Benz himself. Karl actually chose to franchise his operations. He would contract for a specific number of cars, and provided manufacturers with specific serial numbers to use so he could keep track of the amount of cars that were being produced. Although the serial numbers were sequential from one franchiser to the next, there was no guarantee that all numbers were used by the lower numbered manufacture before the next manufacture would start applying their higher numbers. Therefore, the serial number on a particular car did not indicate its order of production. Below is a photograph of an original sales brochure from 1900 for Hewetson's Limited, the exclusive manufacturer and dealer for Benz for the Great Britain area.

Karl Benz made a handful of design improvements on the Model 1 when he created the Velo. The most notable would probably be the addition of a fourth wheel to allow for more stability when turning. The Velo, similar to its predecessor, also has

a single cylinder engine. However, advancements were made to increase its power to one and a half horsepower. Additionally, a two speed transmission was added to this newer model, which utilized two flat belts with levers to allow the driver to shift from one belt system to the other instead of using one belt to control both systems. Benz also decided to reduce the size of the flywheel, which enabled his flywheel engine design to be rotated 90 degrees. The clear advantage to having the flywheel in a vertical, as opposed to horizontal position, enabled the crank shaft to receive better lubrication with its new horizontal positioning.

You may have noticed already that neither of these early Benz models rely on a radiator to cool its engine. This is actually another practical innovation that Karl Benz added to his Velo. The photograph below displays a long copper saddle tank on the upper right side. There is another saddle tank on the

opposite side of the car. A tube runs between these two tanks to ensure that the coolant level of the tanks remains equal at all times. Coolant is drained from this tube onto the engine to prevent it

from overheating. As soon as the coolant hits the engine, the heat vaporizes it into a steam. The vaporized coolant is captured through another tube that leads to a condenser that is located behind the seat. The condenser then changes the steam back into liquid and feeds it back into the saddle tanks for reuse.

It is believed that there are six 1895 Benz Velos left in existence today. Of the six, two are currently located in San Diego, California. When visitors of the J.A. Cooley Museum see this rare vehicle, they often ask, "Does it still run?" Jim Cooley, with passenger Ed Meanley, provide a first hand response to that question below:

1899 Mobile

As mentioned before, around the turn of the century, many innovators were experimenting with different sources of power for self-propelled forms of transportation. The 1899 Mobile is a steam powered automobile that was built by Cosmopolitan Magazine publisher, John Walker. Walker and his business partner Anzi Barber purchased the patents for the steam mobile from the Stanley Brothers. Walker and Barber had several disagreements, which ultimately led to them going their separate ways. Walker started his own company, the Mobile Automobile Company, while Barber continued producing automobiles using the Locomobile name. A couple years after this, the Stanley Brothers began infringing upon these patents by producing their Stanley Steamer car. Instead of fighting with the Stanley Brothers in court, Walker and Barber sold the patents back to them. For this reason, there are extremely small differences between the Mobile, the Locomobile, and the Stanley Steamer. Essentially, they are all the same car!

There are some drawbacks to the steam powered automobiles, such as the Mobile. It takes approximately thirty minutes to build up sufficient steam to start the car, whereas the gasoline powered engine offers the convenience of instant power. In studying these early steam powered vehicles, Jim Cooley believes that steam powered vehicles could have been a viable option for transportation had they benefited from the same amount of research and development as the gasoline engine. The oil and gas

1900 Crest

suppliers during this time were motivated to support the development of the far more expensive gasoline powered engine.

The 1900 Crest is another example of the early gasoline powered cars from this era. It has a single cylinder, 3 1/2 horsepower engine that sits out in front of the car. This particular vehicle is an extremely original car, and very few are left in existence today. Its rarity is due in part to the fact that the following year the body style for this vehicle changed along with its name, to Crestmobile. This vehicle even has its original tires, which are unique because they are single tubed tires. Think of these tires as inner tubes that are about 3/8 of an inch thick, and have no beads on the wheel. This makes traveling at fast speeds somewhat difficult because the tires would often roll off the rim, especially on a turn. Usually this does not result in a flat tire, but it does create the added hassle of frequent stops to remount the tires.

As noted with its body style, the 1900 Crest is really not much more than a horse drawn carriage itself. If you remove the engine mounted in the front, you are practically left with a carriage set to be pulled by horses. For its time, it was not known for its durability, which is most likely a large contributor to this automobile company having to close its doors in 1905. An original photograph of the 1900 Crest in the Cooley Collection can be seen on the following page.

1903 Curved Dash Oldsmobile

Ransom E. Olds built his first car in 1897, but he did not start production until 1901. The Curved Dash is the first mass produced automobile in the United States. With more speed, more reliability, and more durability, it upstaged other car models during this time, like the 1900 Crest, by far. The 1903 Curved Dash Oldsmobile Model R was one of the most popular vehicles of its time. It has a one cylinder, water cooled, 4 1/2 horsepower engine and a planetary, two speed transmission. During the release of this Oldsmobile, the two speed transmission was widely popular because it offered two forward gears and one reverse, which made maneuverability much easier than other single speed transmissions.

The 1901 Oldsmobile is also known as the "Curved Dash" because Ransom Olds was more concerned with the mechanical design of his car than the appearance. He developed his car with the engine at the rear, transmission under the seat, and left the design for the front of the car up in the air. His quick solution was to curve the sheet metal up and back to get it out of the way. He liked the appearance, so it became the famous "Curved Dash."

From 1901 through 1905, over 19,000 were produced. A great deal of its success was in part due to it being a simple car that was easy to operate even for the non-mechanically minded consumers. A new feature of this automobile was that the engine would splash oil downward towards the ground instead of the upward motion that had been used by other cars. This made the 1903 Olds popular with women in particular because they were able to get from here to there and still look presentable. While it may seem like a small convenience, it sparked quite the social movement. Females for the first time were consumers of the automobile able to purchase and operate this simple vehicle, all on their own.

Additionally, its popularity was only enhanced more by marketing attempts. Most famously, the successful tune "Come   with me Lucille In My Merry Oldsmobile"

was a wildly popular song in its day boasting the lyrics:

"...He'll win Lucille with his Oldsmobile,
And then he'll fondly croon, Come away with me Lucille
In my merry Oldsmobile,
Down the road of life we'll fly
Automobubbling, you and I,... You can go as far as you like
with me In my merry Oldsmobile..."

Another clever marketing attempt that enhanced the popularity of the vehicle was a cross country road trip. This highly publicized road trip showed consumers the reliability and durability that this vehicle could offer, being able to sustain some of the roughest road conditions for an extended period of time.

It is hard to imagine that this widely popular vehicle almost did come to exist. In 1901, there was a disastrous fire in the Oldsmobile factory, which destroyed all of the blueprints. Luckily, the only thing that escaped the flames was the prototype for the Runsabout model thanks to a quick-thinking young worker that pushed one of the models out the door before the factory and its content burnt to the ground.

In 2004, General Motors ended production of its last line of Oldsmobile, which marked the end of the oldest car company in America at the time.

1905 Cadillac Model F

1906 Cadillac Model K

Now that the automobile industry had established that they could mass produce reliable gasoline powered vehicles, it was time to take the automobile to the next level. And who better to do that than Cadillac? The Detroit Automobile Company was founded by a group of investors and Henry Ford around the turn of the century. Unable to drive results, Henry Ford was forced to step down as CEO in 1902. Ford went on to start another automobile company, while Henry Leland was chosen to replace him. Leland's first move was changing the name of the company to Cadillac, the name of one of his ancestors, Antoine Laumet de La Mothe sieur de Cadillac, who founded the city of Detroit.

In 1903, Henry Leland produced the first Cadillac, which was designed and engineered by Alanson Brush. Brush's 1903 Model offered a 6 horsepower 1 cylinder engine. Henry Leland advanced this design in 1904 with an 8 horsepower single cylinder engine. This new model was produced until 1909 with little changes made to the design over the years. Alanson Brush left Cadillac and went to work for Henry Ford for a brief period of time. For this reason, you can see Brush's design influence with the striking resemblance between the 1903 Ford Model A and the 1903 Cadillac Model A.

Cadillac's most significant contribution to the development of the automobile was the introduction of standardization. In other words, interchangeable parts. Before standardization, if you broke a piston rod or any other mechanical part on a car, you would have to find a blacksmith to repair it, or a machine shop to make a new part. It could take months to get the parts needed to repair your vehicle. With standardization, there were replacement parts available for purchase. You could cut the repair time of your vehicle down to an hour or two.

In order to achieve recognition for his ability to produce interchangeable parts, Henry Leland sent three of his one cylinder Cadillacs to England as candidates for the prestigious Dewars Trophy. The cars were completely disassembled, the parts were scrambled, and then, the three vehicles were reassembled. The final test was to drive the cars on a test track for one hundred miles at an average speed of thirty-five miles per hour. The cars performed remarkably, and became the first American car to win this award.

Currently, the Cooley Collection has three Cadillacs. The earliest of which is a 1905 Model F, which has never been restored. It is believed that this particular vehicle had been owned by Ira Copley, the founder of Copley Press. In addition to this, the Collection also houses a 1906 Cadillac Model K. Like other vehicles in the Collection, this car has close ties to San Diego.

Don Lee owned several Cadillac dealerships in California. He purchased this vehicle in Pasadena, and kept it on display at his dealerships. One of his top salesman, Marvin K. Brown, decided to purchase one of Don Lee's dealerships in San Diego. Mr. Brown also purchased this vehicle so he could display it as well at his new dealership. Over the years, this vehicle has been used in numerous dedication ceremonies throughout San Diego,

including the opening of Interstate 5. This vehicle was acquired from Jim Brown, Marvin's son. Above is a photograph of Marvin K. Brown in 1962 at the Interstate 5 dedication ceremony.

The one cylinder Cadillac was so successful that they continued production until 1909, which was quite late for a single cylinder vehicle. In 1905, Cadillac introduced the Model F, which offered more power with a 10 horsepower

1913 Cadillac Model 48

engine. This model had a redesigned body, but still utilized the 1904 chassis. During the period of 1905 through 1909, a number of different models were produced, but no significant engineering changes were made during this period of time.

In 1910, Cadillac became a division of General Motors, with Henry Leland remaining CEO. Since Cadillac had always been a profitable company, his decision to sell out to General Motors was quite perplexing. He remained the CEO of the Cadillac Division until 1917. He stepped down as CEO to begin his own car company, the Lincoln Car Company. After producing 9,800 Lincolns, he sold this company to Henry Ford in 1921. To this end, Henry Ford served as "Book Ends" for Leland's career.

Cadillac had an astonishing amount of engineering advancements that led the industry in technology and development. A good example of one such advancement is the Delco Electrical System developed by Charles Kettering, and later adopted by General Motors in 1912. This system includes an electrical starter and lighting system. This ground-breaking innovation gained international recognition when Cadillac was awarded it's second Dewar Award. No other American car company has been graced with the Dewar Award, let alone graced with it twice! The 1913 Cadillac pictured on the previous page includes the then new Delco Electrical System.

This 1913 Cadillac is believed to be the most original '13 Cadillac left in existence with its original upholstery and paint. When this car was purchased, it was purchased with a complete log from its original date of purchase documenting all changes and services it received over the years. What may be astounding to hear is that this very vehicle has been known to reach top speeds in upward of 80 miles per hour! It was Jim Cooley, himself, that was able to receive such speed during an afternoon ride one day.

In 1915, Cadillac achieved yet another milestone with its introduction of the V8 engine. It offered an astonishing 70 horsepower, which was quite the contrast to the 40 to 48 horsepower engines being offered by the competition. This same year, Cadillac changed to a left-hand drive. Throughout its continued history, Cadillac remained at the top of the industry, having their name synonymous with quality and innovation.

As mentioned previously, Alanson Partridge Brush began his career working for Cadillac, developing their first model before his departure from the company. He then spent a brief period of time at the Pontiac Carriage Company working on the development of the first Oakland. In 1907, he took his years of engineering and design experience with Cadillac, Ford, and Pontiac, and opened his own car company. Brush was able to start production on his vehicles that same year. At this time, one

1907 Brush Model B

cylinder cars were fading in popularity. Regardless, Brush was quite successful, which spoke to his ability to produce a great automobile. Production for the Brush continued through 1912.

The 1907 Brush pictured above was purchased new in San Diego, California, and we have the complete chain of ownership from the first buyer to present. This car was purchased new by a man named Pinkston. He owned the car until he passed away in 1940. We have a copy of the Bill of Sale dated April 26, 1941, signed by all three of his sons. Interestingly, the Bill of Sale noted the car as a 1904, but it is clearly a 1907 since Brush Motor Company did not exist in 1904. Ivan Rawson assumed ownership, and shortly thereafter sold it to Glen Shell, one of the largest antique car collectors in San Diego at the time. After Shell passed away in the 1950s, his entire collection was acquired by Carl Burnett, an antique dealer in San Diego. In 1965, Rawson purchased the car back from Carl Burnett, and sold it again four short years later to a collector named Randall. In 1970, the vehicle was sold again to Jack Wolford, a local historian, who used to manage the bean fields in what is now known as Allied Gardens. He stored the vehicle outside with no cover to protect it from the elements. In 1988, Jim Cooley purchased the vehicle, after Jack's passing. The picture below shows the condition this vehicle had deteriorated into over the years. Jim Cooley then spent several months restoring this vehicle to its current condition today.

1908 Brush Model BA

    The Cooley Collection proudly displays three Brush models, all very similar in their appearance. The three Brushes in the collection all have one cylinder, six horsepower engines. Another common feature among Brushes are their large coil springs. The body of this car hangs off of the springs, which stretches the coil, as opposed to sitting on them, which compresses them. Also, Brush is the first car to feature a counter balanced crank shaft, which significantly decreases the engine vibration into the frame and passenger seat. Early Brush models offered the option of hard rubber or pneumatic tires.

    A trademark characteristic of the Brush automobile is the

large wooden axles it sits on. It may seem like an interesting choice, when considering a steel alternative, but there are several important points that must be considered. The first is that this vehicle is designed to be a slower speed automobile. It is not expected to hit speeds of 60 miles per hour. Also,

the road conditions during that time could cause fatigue on the steel axles causing them to break. The flexibility of wood acts as a better shock absorber, which allows it to outlive its steel counterparts. During its production, the Brush proved to be a reliable and durable vehicle that offered a much smoother ride. True to its marketing slogan at the time, the Brush really was "Every Man's Car."

1910 Brush Model D

Alanson Brush tested his multi-tasking ability when he continued to produce the "Every Man's Car," even after he accepted a position with General Motors (the competition) to head their Buick division. In 1910, Benjamin Briscoe took a stab at giving General Motors some true competition

1908 Maxwell Model RS

by organizing nearly a dozen car manufactures into the United States Motor Company. The idea behind the United States Motor Company was to essentially mirror what General Motors had already done years before. Two of the larger car manufactures that were part of the Unites States Motor Company were Brush and Maxwell. Maxwell was founded in 1904 by Briscoe and Jonathan Dixon Maxwell, who began his career in the automotive industry with Oldsmobile. Maxwells were known as great two cylinder cars. However, in 1912, the United States Motor Company was dissolved after dismal sales performance of its second to last car manufacture, the Brush Motor Company. Maxwell, being the only surviving member of the United States Motor Company, was purchased by Walter Flanders and continued production. Around this time, Maxwell introduced four cylinder models, which it continued to produce until 1925, at which time the company was purchased by the Chrysler Corporation.

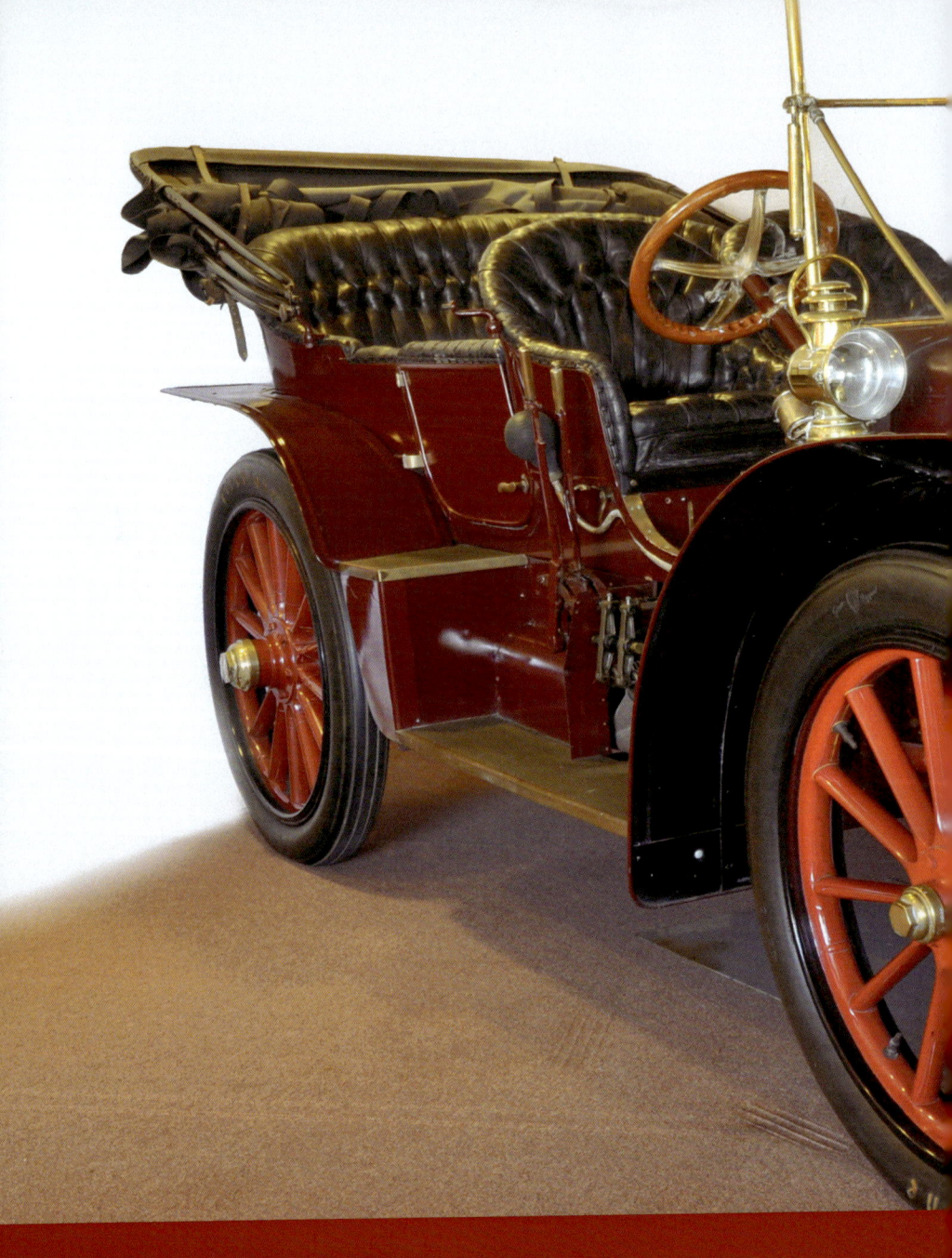

1910 Hu

t Special

With the Cooley Collection housing the best array of 100 year old automobiles, including models such as Benz, Oldsmobile, and Cadillac, to name a few, it may be hard to believe that the 1910 Hunt is truly the centerpiece of this Collection. It is the only vehicle that was actually produced in San Diego, and there was only one ever made. It is truly one of a kind!

William H. Hunt and his brother Clarence were machinists in National City. Following a visit from a representative of the Ford Motor Company in 1904, they became the first car dealer in town. Over the next two years, the brothers only sold one vehicle for Ford, but they were able to create a successful repair business among other ventures. They also hired themselves out as chauffeurs and mechanics.

Clarence Hunt was frequently contracted as a driver by Arnie Babcock, the son of the builder of the Hotel del Coronado, for his trips from Ensenada, Mexico to San Diego, California. Arnie lived 40 miles south of Ensenada, but had frequent meetings and doctor's appointments in San Diego since he suffered from

tuberculosis. These trips took a toll on his cars, so they spent a significant amount of time in the Hunt Brother's repair shop.

In 1908, Arnie commissioned William Hunt to build a vehicle that would be strong enough to endure the rough stretch of road between San Diego and Ensenada. Mr. Hunt designed and machined every inch of this vehicle with the exception of the crank shaft. This vehicle was designed with a powerful double chain drive, an 18" center clearance, and a 60" axle width, to match the width of the ruts in the road. Additionally, Hunt designed the vehicle to have the engine under the front floor boards, being exposed above the running boards. This left the area under the hood completely vacant, and a perfect location for a large water tank to help cool the engine during the hot summer heat.

He called it the Hunt Special, in honor of its creator, but it was nicknamed "Alkali Ike" for it's ability to navigate one of the toughest off-road racing areas in the world. Unfortunately, this unique vehicle never served its original purpose. It was completed in 1910, after the deaths of both Clarence Hunt and Arnie Babcock.

However, the vehicle did navigate the roads of Mexico for several years after its completion. It was then placed in storage where it remained until Lonnie Reed purchased it with the intention of bringing this prized vehicle back home to San Diego.

The 1906 REO, contrary to the Hunt, has a body style similar to other manufactures of this era, such as Brush and Maxwell. Not surprising, it also has a single cylinder engine like they do. REO was the second car company started by Ransom E. Olds. As you may remember, he began production of the

1906 REO

Oldsmobile in 1901. In the following years, Ransom gradually sold off shares of his company to interested stockholders. Not long after this, he sold off the majority of his stocks losing the control and decision making power over his own company. His solution was to leave the company in 1904.

He took his experience and automobile knowledge down the street, literally.

He purchased a plot of land, approximately one block from the Oldsmobile factory, and started another car company. Realizing he could not use the Oldsmobile name, he originally named his new company the Olds Motor Company.

1911 REO Truck

Oldsmobile filed suit as it resembled their name too closely. Not wanting the headache, Ransom responded by changing the name of his new company to R.E.O. Motor Car Company, using his initials instead.

While the first REOs produced were one and two cylinder

cars, Ransom quickly realized that the market was changing, and later began producing four cylinder cars. The following page features a picture of the Lansing, Michigan production facility for REO as it appeared on the last page in the Instruction Book accompanying each car sold.

REO received steady sales performance until the Depression. During the Great Depression, it was common for car manufacturers to pool their resources with other car manufacturers which enabled them to continue their operations during this difficult time in history. While the company ended its production of personal cars in 1936, the REO trucks were a different story.

During their early production years, REO had cast a large quantity of one cylinder blocks. This was a common practice for car manufacturers. Since the demand had shifted from one cylinder to four cylinder cars, REO had quite the predicament on their hand as they sat on a large inventory of useless one cylinder blocks. The idea to scrap them was bounced around briefly. However, REO decided to go in a different direction. While the popularity of one cylinder cars had fizzled, it still remained in full steam for one cylinder trucks.

In 1910, the decision was made to use the extra one cylinder blocks to enter the truck market, which they did in 1911. The demand for single cylinder trucks remained for several years longer than that of the car because trucks did not need to go fast. Most were carrying heavy loads and required a slower rate of speed. The REO Truck division is still building trucks today under the Volvo Trucks Division.

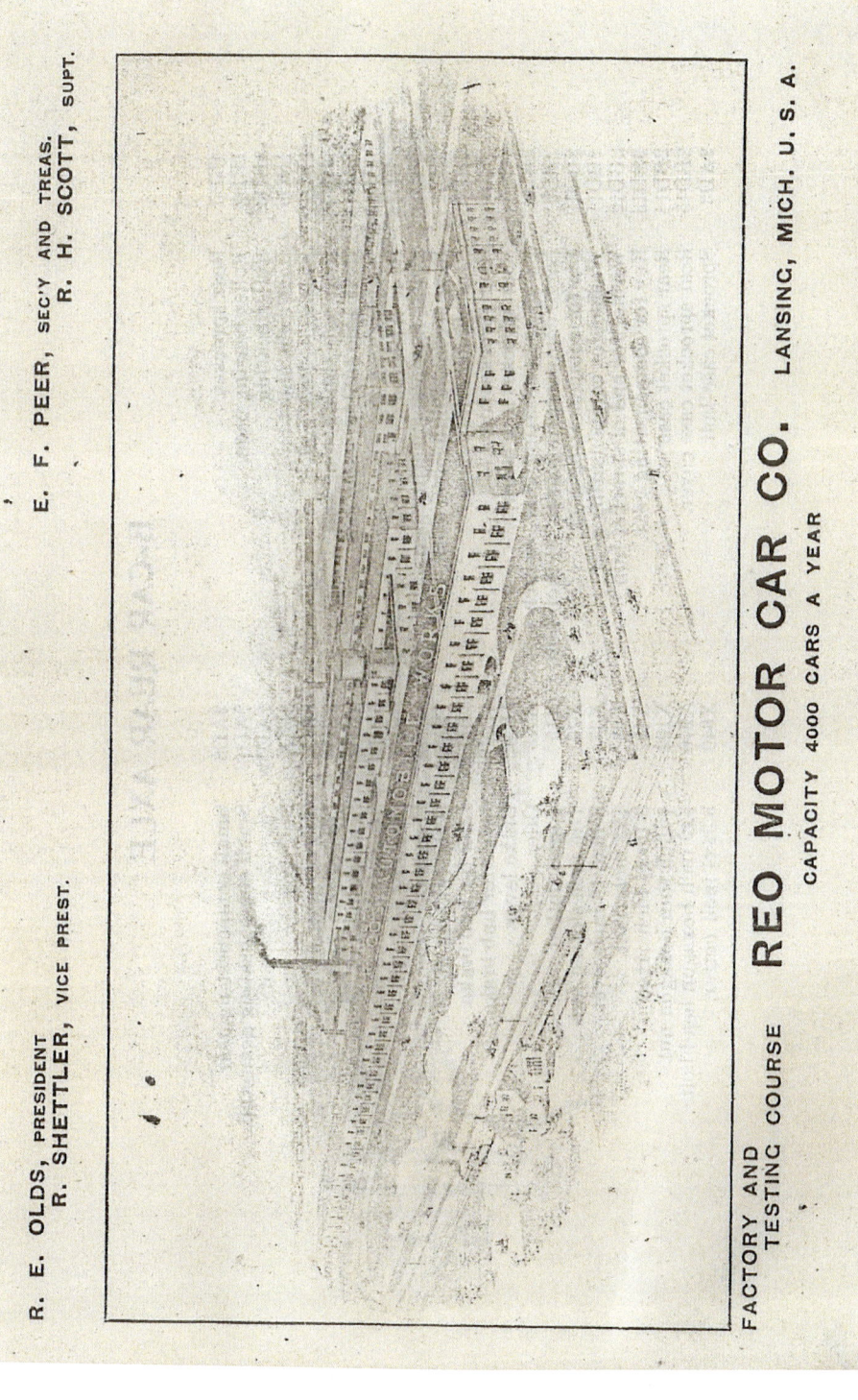

R. E. OLDS, PRESIDENT
R. SHETTLER, VICE PREST.

E. F. PEER, SEC'Y AND TREAS.
R. H. SCOTT, SUPT.

REO MOTOR CAR CO. LANSING, MICH. U. S. A.

FACTORY AND TESTING COURSE

CAPACITY 4000 CARS A YEAR

36

1910 Hudson Model 20

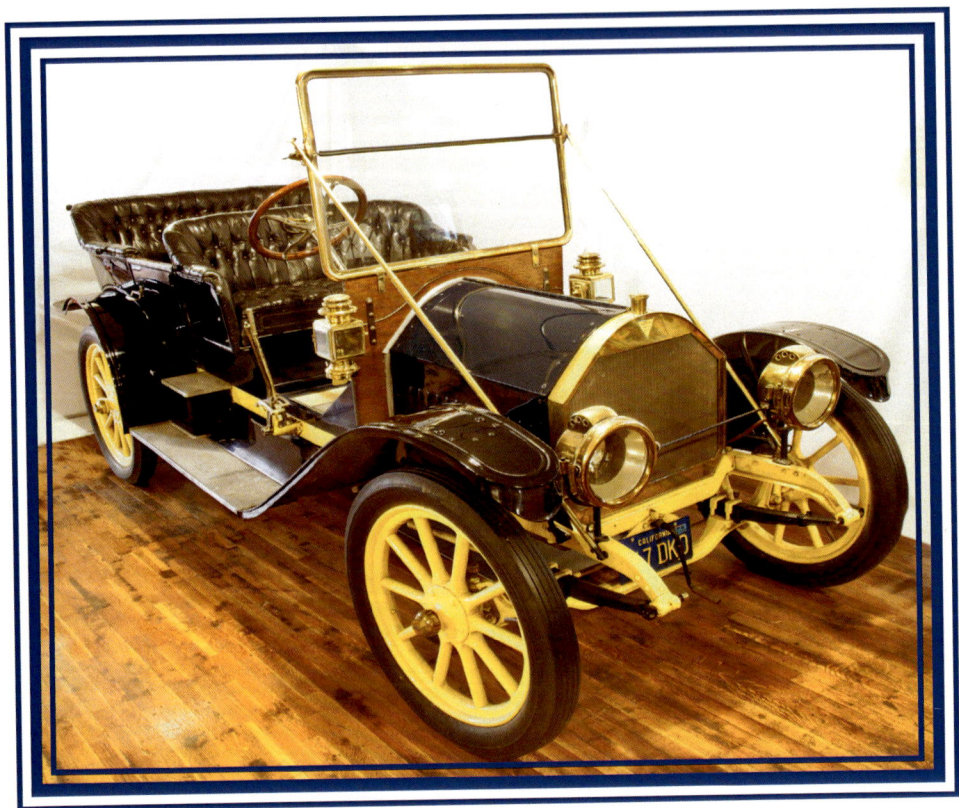

Another, lesser known, automobile manufacturer during this era was the Hudson Motor Car Company, created by Roy Chaplin and financed by J.L. Hudson in 1909. J.L. Hudson made up for any lack of capital with experience. He enlisted six or seven well trained automotive engineers. He was obsessed with engineering design and production quality. This obsession was in contrast to Henry Ford's approach of build them fast and build them cheap.

For instance, Ford continued with planetary transmissions from its beginning until late in the 1920s, while

Hudson offered his first car with a three speed sliding gear transmission. This was one of sixty innovations Hudson introduced into the market with his first vehicle. By 1910, there was a tremendous difference in quality between a Ford and a Hudson. The added quality in a Hudson resulted in a low maintenance vehicle, whereas the Ford Model T was known to breakdown quite often. At that time, the cars had equivalent pricing, but the production numbers for the Hudson were far below that of Ford.

In 1916, Hudson introduced the Model 54, Super Six. With its emphasis on performance, the Super Six enjoyed success in early automotive racing. Hudson set more records before World War I than any other automobile company. Their performance feats continued through the late forties, pioneering the concept of the aerodynamic car, and producing stock cars capable of speeds up to 145 miles per hour.

Along with higher quality and improved performance, Hudson was also the first car company to offer the engine, clutch, and transmission as a single unit. Additionally, it had a mono-block engine, meaning the cylinders were cast into the block. Prior to this, it was common for each cylinder to be cast as a separate part that was bolted onto other engine parts.

Hudson engineering continued into the 1930s with a cushion balanced crankshaft, and a special high compression head that increased the horsepower by 50%. After leading the industry with improvements and innovations, much of which are still used today, the Hudson Motor Company merged with Nash-Kelvinator Corporation in 1954 to become American Motors.

Thus far, we have covered many mainstream contributors to the successful advancements of the automobile industry over the years, and there are plenty more to come. With everything else in life, it is unlikely that you come across the great success of the auto industry without experiencing failure along the way. There are countless car manufacturers that tried, innovated, but did not succeed. The 1914 Woods Mobilette is a great example of the unique attempts that car manufacturers made during their history. It is what is known as a Cycle Car.

Cycle Cars came into being about 1913, and were mainly used in town for small travels, such as running errands or traveling to and from work. They are narrow vehicles requiring tandem seating that offer low horsepower. Most Cycle Cars are four

1914 Woods Mobilette

cylinders and belt driven, with the belts being exposed from the engine all the way to the rear wheels.

All Woods are shaft driven with a differential; none were built with a belt drive. It sits lower than most vehicles with the axles above the frame members. A clear disadvantage to this vehicle is it's impractical turning radius. The wheels only move slightly, so a u-turn takes twice the radius of an 18-wheeler.

Woods Mobilettes were produced in Chicago from 1913 through 1916. They offered their models with various options, such as an air cooled or water cooled engine, and a sliding gear or a friction drive transmission. The Woods Mobilette pictured on the preceding page has a water cooled engine with a sliding gear transmission with three speeds forward and one reverse.

This 1914 Woods Mobilette is in remarkable condition, which is not terribly surprising because for most of its life, it has been stored in museums. While there is a short period of time from 1914 through 1938 that is not documented, it has been housed in three different museums since 1938.

Although undeniably unique, the Woods does have various additional drawbacks related to its narrow bodied design. Due to it's limiting size, this vehicle does not have a water pump, which causes it to overheat frequently, especially on hot days.

When asked about the Woods Mobilette, Jim Cooley fondly reminisces of an experience he witnessed on a Horseless Carriage tour years ago. Another member on the tour was riding in a Woods Mobilette with his blind wife in the rear seat. On one of the mountainous turns the car flipped over on its side. The member safely tended to his wife, escorting her to the side of the road. He then returned to his vehicle with a couple of other members that had stopped. They lifted up the car and righted it back onto its four wheels. The owner then gave the car a crank and it started back up. They finished the tour with nothing more than a couple of scratches on the side of their vehicle.

Practicality is not a strong suit for this vehicle, but it does have a lot of character and will most certainly turn heads, especially considering there are only four known Woods Mobilettes left in existence today.

1904 Michigan

Another lesser known car manufacturer that is featured in the Cooley Collection is the Michigan. Like other automobiles from this era, it is quite small in size. In fact, it is smaller than other one cylinder vehicles, such as Brush, Maxwell, and REO. With its 48 inch wheelbase, the Michigan weighs a whopping 360 pounds! In production from 1903 to 1908 by the Michigan Automobile Company headquartered in Kalamazoo, Michigan. The Michigan Automobile Company was founded at the end of 1902, when brothers, Charles and Frank Fuller, negotiated a deal with another set of brothers, Maurice and Clarence Blood. The Fuller Brothers had experience making washboards and other wood products, while the Blood Brothers were owners of the Kalamazoo Cycle

Company. The Blood Brothers came to the table with some prior experience having just manufactured the Blood Cycle Car. The Model A Michigan was first produced in 1903 featuring a steering lever, like that of the 1903 Curved Dash Oldsmobile, and an air-cooled, single cylinder engine with 3.5 horsepower. A large selling feature of the Michigan was its affordable price tag of $450, one of the cheapest cars at the time, as the sales advertisement below highlights.

While the Michigan is not one of the most recognizable car manufactures in history, it did earn its place in the Cooley Automobile Collection with its contribution to the advancement of automobile. Later models produced by the Michigan Automobile Company are some of the first automobiles in the United States to offer four-wheel drive!

1912 Cartercar

    While the Cartercar may not have as much of a unique appearance as the Woods Mobilette, it offers a distinctively different body. It's papier maché! The car uses compressed papier maché panels over its wood frame for the body of this sedan. The body is approximately seven foot six inches in height. With a four cylinder 30 horsepower engine, during its time, this car was most known for its gearless, friction drive transmission.

    The sedan model of the Cartercar has a unique layout that was used by other car manufacturers during this time. It offers a center door on the sedan for entry into the front or rear seats. The center door design typically has a door on each side of the vehicle that is located just behind the front seats. This arrangement requires the front seat passengers to climb between the two front seat before sitting in their seats. However, this

Cartercar was designed to have the center door on the passenger side, but the door placement on the driver's side was moved up to the driver's seat, providing easy entry for the driver.

In 1905, a gentleman by the name of Byron Carter started his own car company, calling it the Motorcar Company. Located in Jackson, Michigan at the time, he decided to move the operations to Detroit later that year. In 1907, the company would experience another relocation of facilities to Pontiac, Michigan, as well as a name change, to the Cartercar Motor Company. During this time, Byron Carter submitted patents for his friction drive transmission, which became quite the selling point for his vehicles.

Shortly after the name change and third relocation, the Cartercar Motor Company experienced a great loss with the sudden passing of its founder. Byron Carter stopped to assist a stranded female motorist on the side of the road. While attempting to crank start the engine, it backfired causing the crank to hit him in the jaw. The wound eventually became infected, and he died of gangrene shortly thereafter in 1908.

A dear friend of his, Henry Leland, head of Cadillac, was disturbed by his early passing. Some believe that Byron Carter's accidental death from the crank backfiring is what may have inspired Leland to introduce the Delco Electrical System into his 1912 Cadillac, which included a much safer self-starter.

In 1909, General Motors purchased the Cartercar Motor Company, and continued production for several more years. Unfortunately, with disappointing sales numbers, GM decided to discontinue this car line in 1915.

Chevrolet also produced a Sedan model with a similar style to that of the Cartercar. Obviously, it goes without saying, that over the years, Chevrolet has been able to make more of a name for themselves as a power player in the auto industry than Cartercar was ever able to.

In 1911, Louis Chevrolet began producing cars. His first

1918 Chevrolet Model F-40

Baby Grand

models were called "Little." The Little was produced for only a short time, before it was decided to change the name to Chevrolet.

William Durant, the head of General Motors, helped finance Louis Chevrolet's endeavors, consequently adding it as another division of General Motors. During this time, General Motors was still searching for its definition in the auto market. Some of their smaller cars offered a limited line, which eventually became competitive with the Ford. Amid this confusion in 1914, Chevy came out with a larger model carrying the Chevrolet name, the F-40 Model.

This model presented two different body styles. The Royal Mails, as they were called, are roadsters and coupes, whereas the Baby Grands are touring cars and sedans. These cars were designed to sell in the same price range as Buick and Cadillac. The following pages exhibit an excerpt from an original sales catalogue displaying the Baby Grand. The Baby Grand and Royal Mail F-40s continued in production until 1922.

Chevy had an overhead valve engine from its conception, as compared to the Ford's flat head. However, Chevy engines were not as durable as that of Ford's because Ford used vanadium steel, a superior material to Chevy's. Durability aside, the Chevy engines were a more advanced design.

Chevrolet adopted many amenities years before Ford did. By 1915, Chevy had electric lights, an electric generator, and voltage regulator. They benefited from the Delco Electrical System that was introduced by Cadillac, another division of General Motors. Ford did not offer an electrical starter until five years later.

The 1918 Chevy Baby Grand in the Cooley Collection was the first year the company offered a closed car model. After writing to the Chevrolet Division of General Motors, Jim Cooley was able to ascertain that this vehicle is the earliest Chevy Sedan left in existence. The vehicle was found in remarkable condition at a ranch in North Dakota. It had been stored in a barn since 1922, and only had three or four years of service. Cooley's Chevy even has all the original upholstery still intact.

An unusual feature of this car is the windshield. There is a horizontal split in the windshield that permits the upper portion to be rotated outward from its upper edge. Its position is similar to that of a sun visor. The real advantage of this feature is increasing overall visibility when driving in the rain, since Chevy had not introduced windshield wipers on their models yet.

As you can see, these cars have an extremely tall body. A shorter individual could easily move about the cabin of the sedan

CHEVROLET
ENCLOSED MODELS

1918

CHICAGO RETAIL STORES

2612-14 Michigan Ave.   49-51 E. Garfield Blvd.

Used as an open car

Price, $1475 f. o. b.

MODEL
F-A SEDAN

The five-passenger Sedan is entitled to be called a luxurious automobile. And, we do not use the word "luxurious" haphazardly.

The fine coach builder has done his best in designing and building this body. It exemplifies the progress that has been made in building the Sedan type. The stock used is sturdy and lasting.

The driver's individual seat has a three-inch adjustment from the rear of the steering wheel to the back of the seat. This adjustment makes the seat comfortable for any size driver. The right-hand front seat has a tilting back, which is pushed forward on entering or leaving the car. This gives wide clearance when getting in or out.

The side windows drop into pockets, and disappear, with the exception of the two rear windows, which drop down as far as the wheel housing. When a completely open body is desired, the last two are taken out and placed in

Price, $1475 f. o. b. Flint

Used as a closed car

a receptacle, which is located in the back of the rear seat. The back is hinged at the bottom allowing these frames to slide into this compartment easily.

The posts, which are removable, are taken out by releasing thumb nuts at the top of each post, swung into a horizontal position and placed underneath the rear seat, where a receptacle is provided.

The body is mounted on the regular F-A chassis (Baby Grand and Royal Mail models), insuring power for any occasion and mechanical dependability that has been proven beyond question. Thousands of Baby Grand and Royal Mail models are in use today.

The body is fitted with two doors, one on the left-hand side of the driver's seat, and the other on the right-hand side, opening into the tonneau.

The trimming material is of fine-quality cloth. The color is a mixed gray. Colors: black and blue, both rich and durable.

MODEL
F-A SEDAN

standing up. This sedan has another interesting feature. The posts between the side windows and doors can be removed. The side glass is raised and lowered using a leather strap. Thus, in removing the posts and window glass, it is possible to turn the sedan into a touring car

(as displayed in the diagrams from the 1918 sales brochure).

   With its various models offering unique features, Chevy quickly began to outsell Ford, the leader in automobiles at the time. This caused Ford to go back to the drawing board and reinvent their Model T to compete with the models Chevy was producing.

There is one more story to tell before delving into the impact that Ford had on the automobile industry, and that is the story of the Franklin. The Franklin company began in 1902 by Herbert H. Franklin, producing the same model until 1906. These models were known as Cross Engine Franklins because the engine sat crosswise on the frame. In 1906, Franklin turned the engine position 90 degrees to orient it similar to that of other car manufactures. The front grill styling was changed at this time as well to the famous barrel nose Franklin (pictured below). As the name suggests, the front of the vehicle resembled a large circular barrel laying on it's side. This was quite an innovation that completely changed the appearance of the car. Franklin continued with the barrel nose design until about 1912 when they reinvented the whole look of the car by using a new shovel nose look (pictured on Page 52). Their new front grill style became quite famous, and many people visualize the shovel nose design when they hear the name Franklin.

1908 Franklin

The 1918 Franklin in the Cooley Collection, a shovel nose, has a six cylinder, 30 horsepower engine. The H.H. Franklin Automobile Club has confirmed that there are only 2 demi-sedans, such as this one, that are left in existence today. This early series of six cylinder Franklins set a world's record for fuel economy at over 80 miles to the gallon! This record still stands today. It goes without saying that this record was not set by a sedan body style like that of the 1918 Franklin. It was most likely set

1918 Franklin
Model 9B

using a lighter body style, such as a roadster.

The shovel nose design continued production through the early 1920s until they were replaced by the horse collar models. The horse collar was a transition style after the shovel nose. This style was quickly replaced in 1925 with a more conventional looking appearance.

All Franklin cars can be distinguished by their utilization of air cooled engines. They only built cars that have an air cooled engine. Since their engines are air cooled instead of water cooled, there is no need for a radiator, which is what led to some of their early unconventional designs. However, in 1925, they designed their new models using a dummy radiator used solely for aesthetics.

1929 Franklin
Model 135

As you can tell from the 1929 Franklin in the collection that is featured above, the body style of these later Franklins are worlds apart from the earlier design models. The 1929 Franklin is a Model 135 that was purchased new in Pasadena, California. This vehicle was not driven very much at all. It was stored by its second owner in a barn in San Diego, California. Unfortunately, the barn did not have a floor, but rather sat upon a dirt lot. These unfavorable conditions caused this vehicle to grossly deteriorate over time. When removed from the barn, it only had approximately 8,000 miles on it, but it needed much restoration.

The 1929 Franklin is the first model to introduce a steel frame and four wheel hydraulic brakes. This shows how much Franklins tended to lag behind other car manufacturers in terms of technology because most other manufacturers switched to steel frames ten years earlier.

Like all other car companies, Franklin struggled to maintain production through the Great Depression. They took the same approach as their competitors pooling their resources with other car manufacturers to continue production. The 1933 Olympic is a prime example of one of these assembly cars.

Our 1933 Olympic is a three window coupe equipped

1933 Franklin Olympic

with a rumble seat. It has a REO chassis and brakes, and the body is made by a separate body company, such as the Budd Body Company. Essentially the only thing Franklin on this vehicle is its engine and gauges. There is an extremely limited number of these three window coupes that were produced. Exact production numbers are not known, but it is estimated that it was well under a dozen. A few months after releasing the 1933 Olympic, Franklin chose to end its operations in automotive manufacturing to focus exclusively on its aircraft engine division. Franklin continued to produce engines for aircrafts into the 1950s. Franklin's Automotive Division was briefly resurrected in 1948 when they produced

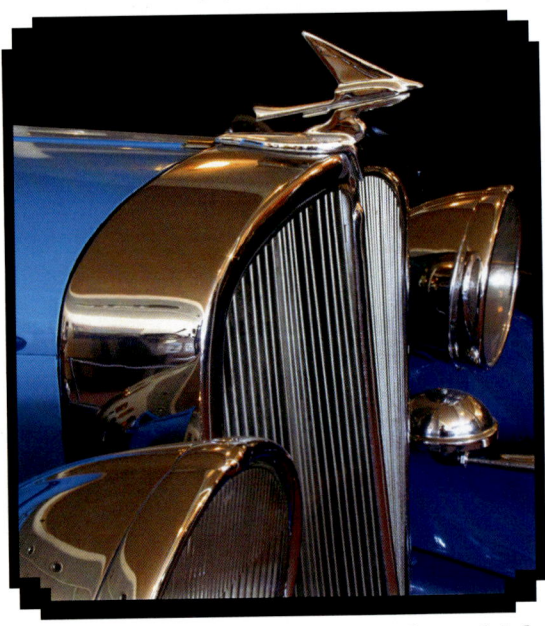

a limited number of Franklin air cooled automobile engines for the Tucker car. This was the last time a Franklin engine was used for automotive applications.

The 1929 and 1933 Franklins in the Cooley Collection are good examples of the trials and tribulations collectors endure during restoration projects. In the case of the 1933 Olympic, Jim Cooley was only able to locate 5 wheels, whereas the vehicle requires six, four on the ground and a spare on each fender. As mentioned, this vehicle is extremely rare. Coming up empty handed on his search for a sixth wheel, Cooley was left with no other choice but to improvise. He realized that Ford made a similar wheel the same year that is approximately the same size. It is nearly perfect with the exception of the bolt pattern and Olympic hubcaps not being compatible. Recognizing this obvious deficiency, Cooley took a spare Olympic hubcap to a local foundry and had them modify it

to allow the back of the Olympic hubcap to fit the smaller sized Ford. This improvisation was needed considering the lack of available parts, yet it is hardly noticeable to an untrained eye.

The restoration of the 1929 Franklin was even more of a headache. Cooley advertised for two years in various trade magazines for 1929 hubcaps. He was able to locate 16 different ones, but not one was presentable enough to be placed on the car. Therefore, the 16 hubcaps were cut down, brazed, and welded back together into 6 good hubcaps.

The hubcaps were not the only thing missing when the 1929 Franklin was acquired. It was also missing a tail light. Cooley advertised for this part for one year before obtaining one from a close friend of his, Rich Alfred. He had placed the tail light in the trunk of his car, a Cadillac, to store until he was able to drop it off at the body shop. A couple days after acquiring this rare, sought after, tail light,

Cooley's car was stolen in broad daylight. He reminisces of that day stating he remembers being more upset about the loss of the tail light in the trunk than he was about losing his Cadillac.

Having to start back at the drawing board, he advertised again in search of another one. Eventually, he was able to locate another tail light. He had to send this one out to be re-plated. The plater destroyed the metal rim of the tail light, shredding it to pieces while trying to buff this fragile part. Devastated by the loss of his second tail light, Cooley was almost certain he would not be able to locate another one after spending over a year and a half locating the first two. He decided to take the remaining pieces of the tail light rim to his personal auto mechanic who then spent the next four days repairing the damages, which are barely noticeable now.

These are just a few of the many stories that can be told regarding the hardships that come along with restoring these old vehicles. It is a far from easy process, but when restoring antique cars, the payoff in the end is almost always worth the headaches you endure during the process.

1926 Ford Model T

    While each of the aforementioned vehicles have contributed to the evolution of the automobile industry, the next vehicle is perhaps the most well-known by the general public, and that is the Ford Model T. As mentioned before, Henry Ford started his career with the Detroit Motor Car Company. After his departure, he sought out several investors to start his own car company, the Ford Motor Car Company.

    In 1903, the company went into production of the Model-A Ford, not to be confused with the 1928 Model A. The

1903 Model A is quite different from Ford's newer models. It is a small two cylinder vehicle, quite similar to the design Alanson Brush used when he worked with Ford at the Detroit Motor Car Company.

1909 Ford Model T

1914 Ford Model T

In 1904, the Ford Motor Car Company produced the Model B, which was a rather primitive four cylinder vehicle. This car turned out to be quite a poor performer, in more ways than one. In 1905, Ford went back to producing the two cylinder design with the Ford Model C.

In 1906, the four cylinder engine was reintroduced in several models, including Model R and Model N. Additionally, a Model K, which offered a six cylinder engine, was introduced this same year. The Model K was an expensive car that was poorly engineered, resulting in unsatisfactory sales. Actually, it almost bankrupted the company. In 1907, the Model K had a slightly improved design, but still lacked in sales performance. This experience most likely alerted Ford to the pitfalls of the expensive car market. Thereafter, he focused his production on small cars that would appeal to the mass market.

The Model N, introduced in 1906, was re-engineered into the slightly improved Model S. Then, in 1908, the Model S was revised again resulting in the Ford Model T, as pictured on pages 59 and 60. The early Model T's have two hand levers and two foot pedals. Shortly after their production, they were recalled to the factory to modify them with a three foot pedal design. This new design remained in production until 1927. The 1909 Ford Model T (pictured on page 59) was the first year this model was produced. This vehicle used to be part of the Cooley Collection.

About this time, Henry Ford visited the Singer Sewing Machine Company, and was intrigued by their assembly line. Singer utilized a moving assembly line powered by a belt from an electric motor. Singer's employees were positioned in front of this belt and assembled parts as they moved by them. This gave Ford the inspiration for his auto assembly line. This method of production is recognized as Ford's greatest achievement.

Another important accomplishment of the Ford Motor Company is the development of vanadium steel, a far superior material than others used in the automobile industry. This durable metal is one reason why Model T's did not suffer from the same problems of other cars, like broken spindles and rods.

Throughout the years, small changes were made to the outward appearance of the Ford Model T, but few changes were made to the mechanics. The Model T was produced through 1927. Throughout its entire life, this car utilized planetary transmissions, whereas most other manufacturers switched to a sliding gear transmission by 1910.

With Chevrolet offering a more modern and better engineered car, they began to outsell Ford in the mid-1920s. The success of Chevrolet was hard for Henry Ford to ignore. He responded by going back to the drawing board and reinventing his famous Model T. In 1928, Ford introduced the Model A, which he coined "The Lady."

Henry Ford shut down his factory for several months retooling his equipment for the production of his new model. The early Model A offered a multiple disk clutch, a powerhouse generator, a removable plate on the oil pan for easy access to the oil pump, and an eighty pound flywheel, to name a few of the upgrades. These features can only be found in the early Model A's, because it was completely redesigned again in 1929. The motivation for the second redesign was likely sparked by a desire to reduce production costs. The redesigned Model A remained in production until 1931.

The 1930 Model A in the Cooley Collection is the fifth car Cooley purchased in his lifetime. With an original purchase price of $50 in the 1940s, Cooley found a vehicle that would last him over seventy years.

1930 Ford Model A

Over these years, Cooley has managed to not only maintain the vehicle, but keeps its original owner's manual too.

He had no intention of buying a collectable at the time of purchase. Rather, he needed something to drive around town. In fact, he still does not see this car as a collectible. It is more like a second vehicle for him. While all of the cars in his collection are in running condition, this is the only vehicle in the collection that he regularly drives today.

The Ford Model T and

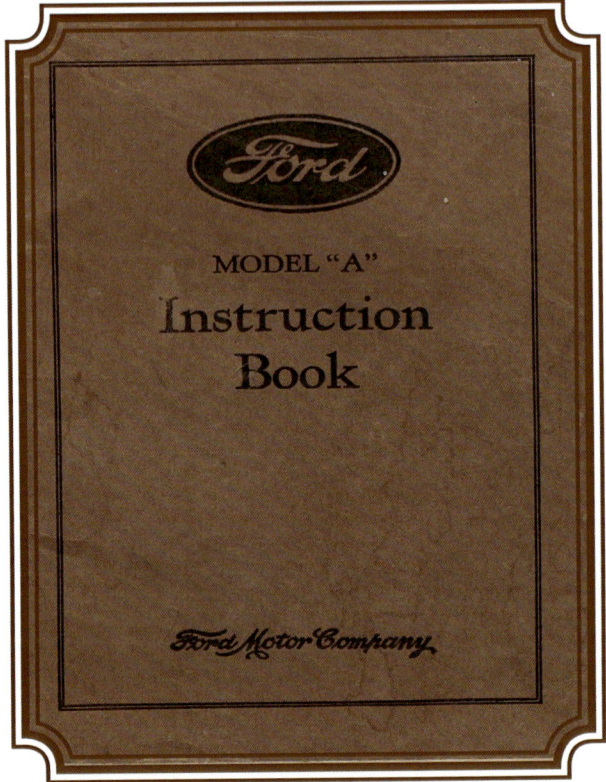

Model A are unique vehicles to have in the Cooley Collection because they did not have a great contribution to the development of the automobile. In fact, they are quite the opposite in the sense that Ford often lagged behind other manufacturers when it came to technological advances. However, Cooley insists that the Ford Model T earned its way into the collection for being the vehicle that put America on wheels. From 1909 through 1927, over 15 million Model T's were produced. No other manufacturers were able to match their production numbers during this time.

Buick
XP 2000

The last automobile to be featured in the Cooley Collection was gifted to Jim Cooley by General Motors. It was conceived by Buick in 1994. It may seem quite odd to have a vehicle this new in the collection, but it serves as a reminder that the automobile industry is not done evolving yet. The '94 Buick is a concept car that never made it into production. After touring the world for various car shows to display what direction the auto industry was taking, the XP 2000 retired at the J.A. Cooley Museum.

The XP 2000 is a fully automated vehicle, so much so that it has the ability to drive itself! Much of the technology introduced by the XP 2000 concept car has now made it into mainstream production, such as park assist, GPS, lane recognition, and back-up sensors, to name a few. The collector himself can attest to this vehicle's ability to drive itself. In the mid-1990s, when Buick was developing this technology they placed sensors in a stretch of highway on Interstate 15. For several months, General Motors used this stretch of highway to test the technology this vehicle was piloting.

One afternoon, General Motors invited Cooley and his wife to the test track to take part in their demonstrations. They were witness to this vehicle's ability to communicate with the road and other vehicles surrounding it in order to change lanes safely, and to accelerate and brake as needed. With the recent technology advancements introduced by the XP 2000, it is clear from these changes that the auto industry is not done developing. The only question left to ask is, what will be next?

The XP 2000 is a fully automated vehicle, so much so that it has the ability to drive itself! Much of the technology introduced by the XP 2000 concept car has now made it into mainstream production, such as park assist, GPS, lane recognition, and back-up sensors, to name a few. The collector himself can attest to this vehicle's ability to drive itself. In the mid-1990s, when Buick was developing this technology they placed sensors in a stretch of highway on Interstate 15. For several months, General Motors used this stretch of highway to test the technology this vehicle was piloting.

One afternoon, General Motors invited Cooley and his wife to the test track to take part in their demonstrations. They were witness to this vehicle's ability to communicate with the road and other vehicles surrounding it in order to change lanes safely, and to accelerate and brake as needed. With the recent technology advancements introduced by the XP 2000, it is clear from these changes that the auto industry is not done developing. The only question left to ask is, what will be next?

assistance. Performed kind deeds. Been generous. Been nice. Showed courtesy. Shared love. A multitude of other gestures would have produced a like response.

But we must be willing to share these expressions to receive them. A lonely life and unnoticed death are unnecessary. Be patient and persistent in seeking out opportunities to unselfishly give of yourself to meet the needs of others. Don't hesitate. "You cannot do a kindness too soon," said Ralph Waldo Emerson, "for you never know how soon it will be too late."

The most terrible poverty is loneliness and the feeling of being unwanted.
MOTHER TERESA

MAKE A DIFFERENCE
IN PEOPLE'S LIVES

Doing nothing for others is the undoing of one's self. We must be purposely kind and generous or we miss the best part of existence. The heart that goes out of itself gets large and full of joy. This is the great secret of the inner life. We do ourselves the most good by doing something for others.

HORACE MANN

A wise and beloved shah once ruled the land of Persia. He cared deeply for his people and wanted only what was best for them. The Persians knew this shah took a personal interest in their affairs and tried to understand how his decisions affected their lives. Periodically he would disguise himself and wander through the streets, trying to see life from their perspective.

One day he disguised himself as a poor village man and went to visit the public baths. Many people were there enjoying the fellowship and relaxation. The water for the baths was heated by a furnace in the cellar, where one man was responsible for maintaining the comfort level of the water. The shah made his way to the basement to visit with the man who tirelessly tended the fire.

The two men shared a meal together, and the shah befriended this lonely man. Day after day, week in and week out, the ruler went to visit the fire tender. The stranger soon became attached to his visitor because he came to where he was. No other person had showed that kind of caring or concern.

One day the shah revealed his true identity. It was a risky move, for he feared the man would ask him for special favors or for a gift. Instead, the leader's new friend looked into his eyes and said, "You left your comfortable palace and your glory to sit with me in this dungeon of darkness. You ate my bitter food and genuinely showed you cared about what happens to me. On other people you might bestow rich gifts, but to me you have given the best gift of all. You have given yourself."

For thousands of years, people have been speculating on what constitutes quality human relationships. With all the philosophies, theories, and speculations, only one principle seems to stand strong. It is not new at all. In fact, it is almost as old as history itself. It was taught in Persia over three thousand years ago by Zoroaster to his fire worshipers. Confucius asserted the principle in China twenty-four centuries ago. In the Valley of Han lived the followers of Taoism. Their leader Lao-Tzu taught the principle incessantly. Five hundred years before Christ, Buddha taught it to his

If you wish others to respect you, you must show respect for them. . . . Everyone wants to feel that he counts for something and is important to someone. Invariably, people will give their love, respect and attention to the person who fills that need. Consideration for others generally reflects faith in self and faith in others.

ARI KIEV

disciples on the banks of the holy Ganges. The collections of Hinduism contained this principle over fifteen hundred years before Christ. Nineteen centuries ago, Jesus taught his disciples and followers much the same principle. He summed it up in one thought: "Do unto others as you would have them do unto you."

Unselfishly giving of ourselves probably wouldn't make it as a primary course of study in the school of success. Although we make a living by what we get, the true rewards are experienced because of what we give. You have not really lived a fulfilled day, even though you may be a success by societal standards, unless you have done something for someone who will never be able to repay you.

In the midst of your flurry of activities in this competitive, go-get-'em world, take a moment for the next several days to reflect on Rabbi Harold Kushner's thoughts: "The purpose of life is not to win. It is to grow and to share. You will get more satisfaction from the pleasure you have brought into other people's lives than you will from the times you outdid and defeated them."

A UNIQUE SPIN
ON GETTING EVEN

During the days of the Berlin Wall, a few East Berliners decided to send their West Berlin neighbors a "gift." They proceeded to load a dump truck with undesirables including garbage, broken bricks, building material, and any other disgusting items they could find. They calmly drove across the border, received clearance, and delivered their present by dumping it on the West Berlin side.

Needless to say, the West Berliners were irritated and intent on "getting even." People immediately began offering ideas on how to outdo the repulsive actions of their adversaries. A wise man interrupted their angry reactions and offered an entirely different approach. Surprisingly, people responded favorably to his suggestions and began loading a dump truck full of essential items scarce in East Berlin. Clothes, food, and medical supplies poured in. They drove the loaded truck across the border, carefully unloaded and

You will find as you look back on life that the moments when you have really lived are the moments when you have done things in a spirit of love.

HENRY
DRUMMOND

Shall we make a new rule of life from tonight: always to try to be a little kinder than is necessary.

JAMES M. BARRIE

stacked the precious commodities, and then left a sign that read, "Each gives according to his ability to give."

Imagine the reaction of those who saw the "payback" and powerful message on the sign. Shock. Embarrassment. Distrust. Disbelief. Maybe even a bit of regret.

What we give to others sends a loud message about who we are. How we respond to unkindness, unfairness, or ingratitude speaks a truckload about our true character.

INFLUENCE

There are little eyes upon you,
And they're watching night and day;
There are little ears that quickly
Take in every word you say;
There are little hands all eager
To do anything you do;
And a little boy who's dreaming
Of the day he'll be like you.

You're the little fellow's idol;
You're the wisest of the wise,
In his little mind about you,
No suspicions ever rise;
He believes in you devoutly,
Holds that all you say and do,
He will say and do, in your way
When he's a grown-up like you.

There's a wide-eyed little fellow,
Who believes you're always right,
And his ears are always open,
And he watches day and night;
You are setting an example
Every day in all you do,
For the little boy who's waiting
To grow up to be like you.

AUTHOR UNKNOWN

NEVER ASSUME
YOU'RE PEDALING TOGETHER

We are born for co-operation, as are the feet, the hands, the eyelids and the upper and lower jaws. People need each other to make up for what each one does not have.

MARCUS
AURELIUS

The definition of the word "cooperation" stems from two Latin words, *co*, meaning "with," and *opus*, meaning "work." So, quite literally, cooperation means working with others. Sounds simple, doesn't it.

For over 25 years the *Des Moines Register* newspaper has sponsored a summer RAGBRAI (Register's Annual Great Bike Ride Across Iowa). Bikers from all over the country emerge on the western side of Iowa determined to be one of hundreds of successful riders who invest a week of their life pedaling their way across the state.

One year RAGBRAI designated our community as a stopping point for the night. It was an incredible sight to watch the bikers swarm into town and set up camp. Young and old alike enjoyed the challenge, fellowship, and fun that accompanied this popular event.

As I walked through one of the camping areas, I overheard a conversation between two riders who were navigating the trail together on a tandem bike. The man was complaining about the difficulty of one of the hills they had to climb earlier in the day. "That was a struggle," he said. "I thought for sure we were going to have to push the bike up the hill on foot."

"It sure was a steep hill," his female companion responded, "and if I hadn't kept the brake on all the way, we would have rolled back down for sure."

There's practically no limit to what people can accomplish when they work cooperatively. However, if just one person drags her feet or continually applies the brake, everyone else suffers. Married couples, work departments, athletic teams, dancers, or the cast in a play need to understand where the team is going, how they will get there, what effort will be required by each person, and what they can do to help each other.

When you're on a tandem bike, you have to pedal together.

The purpose of life is to collaborate for a common cause; the problem is nobody seems to know what it is.
GERHARD
GSCHWANDTNER

NO ONE IS
AN ISLAND

A few years ago I conducted a seminar in Des Moines, Iowa in late October. I arose early in the morning to prepare for the program and was shocked when I turned on the television to see news reports of a premature heavy snowfall in progress. Electricity was out in various parts of the city, numerous traffic accidents had been reported, and no travel was advised.

Later in the day, the no-travel advisory had been lifted so I loaded my vehicle to attempt the trip home. On each side of the freeway that runs through Des Moines were trees loaded with the heavy white snow. I noticed in areas where evergreen trees were close together bowed branches from one tree were resting against the trunk of another, and each tree seemed to be supported by the branches or trunk of another tree.

Where trees stood alone, the heavy snow had caused tremendous damage. The branches were unable to handle the heavy weight and, without the support of other trees, they had snapped. Thousands of small and large branches painted the white landscape. Seedlings and strong mature trees were irreparably damaged.

We are not unlike those trees. When the premature, unexpected, or normal storms of life hit, we need the support of other people to withstand the weight of the burden. Human beings aren't designed to stand on their own, and the closer we grow together, the more mutual support we can provide.

FOOTSTEPS

A careful man I ought to be;
A little fellow follows me.
I do not dare to go astray
For fear he'll go the selfsame way.
Not once can I escape his eyes;
Whate'er he sees me do he tries.
Like me he says he's going to be—
That little chap who follows me.
I must remember as I go
Through summer sun and winter snow,
I'm molding for the years to be—
That little chap who follows me.

AUTHOR UNKNOWN

LOVE

There is little doubt that most of us
long for stronger, more creative and rewarding
ways of loving each other.

LEO F. BUSCAGLIA

GOOD ADVICE . . .
WRONG APPLICATION

A couple engaged to be married began experiencing difficulties in their relationship. The constant conflict caused them to question their wedding plans. The man, concerned he could lose the woman he loved, realized there were many unresolved issues he had no idea how to handle. So he sought the advice of a counselor who suggested the problems could be solved if he would take up biking. "I want for you to ride ten miles a day for the next two weeks and then check back with me." Two weeks went by and the man reported back to his counselor as requested. "So, how are you and your fiancee doing now?" the counselor inquired. "How should I know," the man replied, "I'm 140 miles away from home and haven't talked to her for 14 days."

There will always be challenges and problems in any relationship. No problem! Dr. Theodore Rubin advises in *One to One:* "The problem is not that there are problems. The problem is expecting otherwise and thinking that having problems is a problem."

I like long walks, especially when they are taken by people who annoy me.

FRED ALLEN

Abundant advice is available from assorted sources for anyone wishing to enrich his or her relationships. Unfortunately, none of that advice is worth a plugged nickel unless you're willing to step up your investment in people.

My advice: (1) Remember that creating and nourishing relationships is hard work; (2) there will always be problems; (3) relationships are worth every ounce of effort it takes to work through the unavoidable challenges.

This is good advice, if I must say so myself. Apply it—NOW.

CREATE YOUR EMOTIONS
THROUGH YOUR MOTIONS

D r. Joyce Brothers tells the story of a judge trying to change the mind of a woman filing for divorce. "You're 92," he said. "Your husband is 94. You've been married for 73 years. Why give up now?" "Our marriage has been on the rocks for quite a while," the woman explained, "but we decided to wait until the children died."

Dr. Robert Taylor, author of the book *Couples: The Art of Staying Together,* said, "We're now living in the age of disposability: Use it once, and throw it away. Over the past decade, there has developed a feeling that relationships are equally disposable."

The throw-away culture in which we live seems intent on throwing out the principle that marriage is a commitment requiring effort.

According to a *U.S. News and World Report* study, the single biggest reason couples split up is the "inability to talk honestly with each other, to bare their souls, and to treat each other as each other's best friend." The same factors continue to rank high on the list of reasons for marriage breakups.

Happy marriages begin when we marry the ones we love, and they blossom when we love the ones we marry.

TOM MULLEN

On the dance floor, as in life, you're only as good as your partner.

ROBIN MARANTZ HENIG IN *USA TODAY*

Here's a familiar scenario: Your spouse complains, "You never tell me you love me anymore." You take the hint and mumble, "Of course I love you." But inside you're thinking, "Silly, I wouldn't be living with you if I didn't love you. But if anything changes, you'll be among the first to know." Why don't we just respond with a warm kiss and then say, "I'm sorry I haven't told you lately how much I love you."

The great psychologist Dr. George W. Crane said in his famous book, *Applied Psychology,* "Remember, motions are the precursors of emotions. You can't control the latter directly but only through your choice of motions or actions. . . . To avoid this all too common tragedy (marital difficulties and misunderstandings) become aware of the true psychological facts. Go through the proper motions each day and you'll soon begin to feel the corresponding emotions! Just be sure you and your mate go through those motions of dates and kisses, the phrasing of sincere daily compliments, plus the many other little courtesies and you need not worry about the emotion of love. You can't act devoted for very long without feeling devoted."

When we treat our spouse as the most important person in our life, we will begin feeling it, believing it, and enjoying it. What can you do this week to turn "motions into emotions"?

TO MY GROWN-UP SON

My hands were busy through the day
I didn't have much time to play
The little games you asked me to.
I didn't have much time for you.
I'd wash your clothes, I'd sew and cook,
But when you'd bring your picture book
And ask me please to share your fun,
I'd say: "A little later, son."
I'd tuck you in all safe at night
And hear your prayers, turn out the light,
Then tiptoe softly to the door.
I wish I'd stayed a minute more.
For life is short, the years rush past.
A little boy grows up so fast.
No longer is he at your side,
His precious secrets to confide.
The picture books are put away,
There are no longer games to play,
No good-night kiss, no prayers to hear.
That all belongs to yesteryear.
My hands, once busy, now are still.
The days are long and hard to fill.
I wish I could go back and do
The little things you asked me to.

AUTHOR UNKNOWN

WHAT DOES LOVE LOOK LIKE?

What does love look like? It has the hand to help others. It has the feet to hasten to the poor and needy. It has the eyes to see misery and want. It has the ears to hear the sighs and sorrows of men. That is what love looks like.

SAINT
AUGUSTINE

Much has been written "about" love but maybe we've been short-sighted in helping people understand "how to" love. I know this is elementary, but love is more than hugs, kisses, and affection. It also transcends the emotional feeling so many consider love. Love is demonstrated by an attitude of sensitivity and concern and is expressed through sincere actions. Then, the emotion of love surfaces and grows from there.

Let me make this simple. "You can't put a price tag on love," said Melanie Clark, "but you can on all its accessories." Activating the "accessories" of love requires us to eliminate the baggage of pettiness, jealousy, resentment, and judgment. Just love. Think and behave as if you love. By loving thinking and loving actions, we expand our ability to express authentic love. Remember, the emotional part of love is achieved when the thinking and acting are activated.

Maybe a few real-life examples will clarify the "how to" for loving and encourage you to show the accessories of love:

A Welsh gentleman fell in love with one of his neighbors and wanted to marry her. The couple got into an argument and she refused to forgive. The man was shy and hesitated to face his love. Instead, he slipped a love letter under her door every week.

Finally, after 42 years, he worked up the courage, knocked on her door, and asked her to become his wife. To his surprise, she said yes. The couple was married at age 74.

Although his approach was a bit unconventional, it was a determined display of persistent love. What are you doing every week to show those you love how much they mean to you?

I've enjoyed attending the entertaining musical play *Fiddler on the Roof* many times. In one scene, Tevye, seeing the example of his daughters, begins to think about love as a basis for marriage. So after years of marriage, he asks his wife, "Do you love me?" She replies, "For 25 years I washed your clothes, slept in your bed, bore your children, and fixed your meals. If that isn't love, what is?" But Tevye persists: "Do you love me?" After repeated requests, Tevye's wife was only able to respond, "I suppose I do."

"Do you love me?" In the ideal world, this question would be unnecessary. In the real world, countless people yearn to hear the words "I love you."

Ida Fay Oblesby, writing in the *P.E.O. Record* (January 1983), tells the story of an eight-year-old girl in a Pennsylvania orphanage who was shy, unattractive, and regarded as a problem. Two other asylums had her transferred, and now this director was seeking some pretext for getting rid of her. One day, someone noticed the little girl was writing a letter. An ironclad rule of the institution was that any communication from a child had to be approved before it was mailed. The next day, the director and her assistant watched the child steal out of the dormitory and slip down to the main gate. Just inside the gate was an old tree with roots showing above the ground. They followed and watched as the child hid the letter in one of the crevices of the root. Carefully looking around, the little girl scurried back to the dormitory.

The director took the note and tore it open. Then, without speaking, she passed the note to her assistant. It read, "To anybody who finds this: I love you."

What a powerful message from the hearts of those hungry to have someone to love and love them back.

Alvin Straight lived a few miles from me in Laurens, Iowa. His brother, age 80, lived several hundred miles away in Blue River, Wisconsin. According to local news reports, Alvin's brother had suffered a stroke, and Alvin wanted to see him, but had no transportation. Alvin's eyesight wasn't good enough to have a driver's license, and he refused to take a plane, train, or bus. So Alvin, at age 73, climbed aboard his 1966 John Deere tractor lawn mower and drove it all the way to Blue River, Wisconsin. Now that's devotion.

People's needs are not inconveniences, irritations, or a disruption to our comfortable lifestyles. Needs are opportunities to share a portion of ourselves, to stretch our ability to give, and to sharpen our ability to become others-minded.

The following appeared on the editorial page of the *Pasadena Star News* in November of 1985:

Just about everyone knows the Jim Brady story—the man who, only two months after becoming White House press secretary, was shot in the head during the attempted assassination of President Reagan, and how he has fought his way back from brain surgery and the crippling, enduring damage from the stray bullet. However, not many people know, however, about the ceaseless, selfless, devoted love of Bob Dahlgren . . . a man who loved Brady like himself.

A few months ago, Bob Dahlgren died in his sleep, at 52 years of age. It didn't even make the morning news. But during the long months following the shooting, it was

Dahlgren who kept the vigil with Brady's wife, Sarah, through the long series of brain operations.

It was Dahlgren and his wife, Suzie, who took Brady's young son Scott into their home through the early days of the ordeal. It was Dahlgren who arranged the happy hours with Brady's friends by his hospital bedside. As Brady recovered and returned to a semi-normal life, it was always Dahlgren who scouted out the advance arrangements, who helped load and unload his friend from the specially equipped van in which Brady did most of his traveling. It was Dahlgren who helped Sarah field the questions about Brady's health and spent endless hours keeping friends posted on his condition. It was Dahlgren who helped organize a foundation to assure financial support for the family.

For more than four and a half years after Brady was shot, Bob Dahlgren devoted virtually all his time to the man he loved. And he did so with little recognition and no hint of seeing anything in return. Never, ever did Dahlgren complain. Never did he hesitate when needed. Never did he stop looking for the needs or the response of love.

As Dr. Arthur Kobrine, the surgeon who lived through Brady's long ordeal with him, once said, "Everyone should have a friend like Bob Dahlgren."

I read a story in *Our Daily Bread* about a king who had a silver bell placed in a high tower of his palace early in his reign. He announced that he would ring the bell whenever he was happy so that his subjects would know of his joy.

The people listened for the sound of that silver bell, but it remained silent. Days turned into weeks, and weeks into months, and months into years. But no sound of the bell rang out to indicate that the king was happy.

The king grew old and gray, and eventually he lay on his deathbed in the palace. As some of his weeping subjects gathered around him, he discovered that he had really been loved by his people all through the years. At last the king was happy. Just before he died, he reached up and pulled the rope that rang the silver bell.

Think of it—a lifetime of unhappiness because he didn't know that he was warmly loved and accepted by his loyal subjects.

Many people live out their days without the joy of knowing or experiencing the love of others. This book is filled with ideas, illustrations, and inspiration for showing others what love looks like. Give them a try.

Love is like a beautiful flower which I may not touch, but whose fragrance makes the garden a place of delight just the same.

HELEN KELLER

THE FLIP SIDE
OF LOVE

Our lives are shaped by those who love us—by those who refuse to love us.

JOHN POWELL, S.J.

I love to watch reruns of old television series such as the *Andy Griffith Show.* Unlike many of today's programs, the oldies seem to contain a practical, life-enhancing message. In one of the first segments, Sheriff Andy Taylor decides to invite his spinster Aunt Bee to come and live with Opie and him. Following the death of his wife, Andy thought Aunt Bee would add the missing feminine touch to their home.

Opie doesn't share Andy's sentiments and is skeptical of having Aunt Bee coming to "replace" his mother. Andy devises a plan to help Opie accept the idea. He invites Aunt Bee to go fishing and frog catching with them so that Opie will have a chance to get to know her and, it's hoped, bond with her. Unfortunately, Aunt Bee fails miserably at fishing, can't catch a frog, and later reveals her lack of football skills.

Late that night, after Opie is in bed, Aunt Bee talks Andy into taking her to the bus station. Opie hears her crying beneath his bedroom window and realizes she is probably leaving. He jumps out of bed, runs downstairs and out to the truck, exclaiming, "We can't let her go, Pa; she needs us. She can't even catch frogs, take fish off the hook, or throw a football. We've got to take care of her or she'll never make it."

Love springs to life when we realize the benefit of our relationships is not what we will receive from someone else. We need other people because of our weaknesses, and they need us to complement their lives by infusing our strengths with their weaknesses. The process for creating healthy, mutually beneficial relationships unveils a realization that love is best expressed when we fill in the void in someone's life and by doing so expand the value of our own lives.

Although Sheriff Taylor acted on a pure motive of wanting a feminine touch in their home, it was Opie who delivered the punch line, "We've got to take care of her or she'll never make it." Although love may not be reciprocated by those we give it to, our lives will not remain the same when we commit to filling the vacuum in others' lives. "Love cures people," said Karl Menninger, " both the ones who give it and the ones who receive it."

Love has nothing to do with what you are expecting to get—only what you are expecting to give—which is everything. What you will receive in return varies. But it really has no connection with what you give. You give because you love and cannot help giving. If you are very lucky, you may be loved back. That is delicious but it does not necessarily happen.
KATHARINE
HEPBURN

FORGIVENESS

He that cannot forgive others
breaks the bridge over which he must pass himself;
for every man has need to be forgiven.

THOMAS FULLER

KEEP YOUR BRIDGES
IN GOOD REPAIR

An army general once said to John Wesley, "I never forgive and I never forget." John Wesley answered, "Then, sir, I hope you never sin."

I feel sorry for this general. He probably never experienced the load-lifting action of forgiveness. To forgive someone means to let go. Once you forgive, the emotional baggage from tension, unresolved conflicts, or mistreatment is lifted. Robin Casarjian, author of *Forgiveness: A Bold Choice for a Peaceful Heart,* who managed to forgive the man who raped her, said, "Once you forgive, you are no longer emotionally handcuffed to the person who hurt you." What freedom!

"You have a tremendous advantage over the person who slanders you or does you a willful injustice," declared Napoleon Hill. "You have it within your power to forgive that person."

Are you angry with someone who has offended you? Let it go. The anger only pulls you down. Forgiveness provides you the power to get on with life.

Do you carry grudges? Grudges are simply a buildup of resentment produced by an unwillingness to genuinely forgive. We can't "bury the hatchet" with the handle sticking out.

Have you ever said, "I'll forgive but I can't forget?" That is only superficial forgiveness allowing us to continue wallowing in self-pity. The quickest way to forget is to quit dwelling on the wrong done to you.

The American Red Cross was founded by a pioneering woman named Clara Barton, who was widely known for her forgiving spirit. On one occasion a friend brought up an injustice done to her years before. When Barton failed to respond to the effort to relive this event, the friend persisted, "Don't you remember how much that person hurt you?"

"No," Clara Barton cheerfully responded. "I distinctly remember forgetting that."

To proactively forgive the past, quit dwelling on the hurt. By not reliving the situation over and over, you will gain peace and victory over the incident.

If you want to maintain the bridges that sustain relationships but sense some repair work is needed, consider these suggestions.

1. Be the First to Ask Forgiveness. Whether you have hurt someone or been mistreated, be the first to say, "Please forgive me if I've done anything to hurt our relationship." This action will allow you to let go and get on with your life.

2. Rebuild Your Thoughts. The mind is a marvelous mechanism. The thoughts we hold in this massive human computer will dominate our lives. Although not an easy task, discipline yourself not to dwell on the situation or the bitterness, blame, or hurt that can saturate the walls of your mind.

3. Pray. I am rarely capable of genuine forgiveness without divine intervention. Relying on God to help me deal with the pain, the person, and the process of healing replaces the human tendency of revenge with release.

4. Write a Letter. Expressing your feelings in writing, without placing judgment or blame, can be a significant bridge from pain to peace. Simply communicating your heart signals a desire to achieve resolution. Whether or not you ever send the letter, writing it contains its own value.

5. Focus on the Future. Wallowing in the mire of the past destroys the bridge to the future. Tomorrow can never be lived to the fullest when we are consumed with the uncontrollable past.

Elbert Hubbard wrote, "A retentive memory may be a good thing, but the ability to forget is the true token of greatness. Successful people forget. They know the past is irrevocable. They're running a race. They can't afford to look behind. Their eye is on the finish line. Magnanimous people forget. They're too big to let little things disturb them. They forget easily. If anyone does them wrong, they consider the source and keep cool. It's only the small people who cherish revenge. Be a good forgetter. Business dictates it, and success demands it."

Forgiveness allows you to be free from the nightmares of the past and to reclaim your dreams for the future.

6. *Replace Selfishness with Unconditional Love.* Old Pete was in bad health and death seemed imminent. For years there had been a thorn of bitterness with Joe, formerly one of his best friends. Wanting to clear the air, Pete sent word for Joe to come and see him.

When Joe arrived, Pete told him that he couldn't live another day or face eternity knowing their relationship had been destroyed. Pete painfully and reluctantly apologized for the hurtful things he had said and done. He also assured Joe that he forgave him for his actions. The two old friends shook hands and everything seemed fine until Joe turned to go. As he turned to leave, Pete said, "If I get better, none of this counts."

Saying "I forgive you" and then placing conditions on our forgiveness equates with not forgiving at all. It's tough to remove our selfish motives and refrain from resurrecting past grievances when frictions arise.

I'm reminded of the lady who sought marriage counseling. The counselor asked her what seemed to be the source of their difficulty. "Whenever we get into an argument," the lady said, "my husband becomes historical."

"Don't you mean hysterical?" the counselor responded.

"No, I mean historical! He always brings up the past."

Emotional problems and relational stress will continue as long as forgiveness hinges on the past. Total forgiveness requires unconditional love.

I hope your relationships will continue to mature and reap positive results. A forgiving spirit is a basic requirement for that to occur. Forgiveness remains the bridge we must cross to enter brighter tomorrows. Remember the words of Martin Luther King, Jr.: "Forgiveness is not an occasional act; it is a permanent attitude."

Ninety percent of the art of living consists of getting along with people you cannot stand.
SAMUEL GOLDWYN

In *The Essential Calvin Hobbes,* the cartoon character Calvin says to his tiger friend, Hobbes, "I feel bad that I called Susie names and hurt her feelings. I'm sorry I did it."

"Maybe you should apologize to her," Hobbes suggests.

Calvin ponders this for a moment and replies, "I keep hoping there's a less obvious solution."

There's no easy way of saying "I'm sorry, I was wrong." Do it anyway. Rather than allowing bitterness and resentment to surface, allow the sweet smell of harmony to be the trademark of your relationships.

PLACING PEOPLE
IN PROPER PERSPECTIVE

B arbara Bush was not Wellesley College's first choice as their 1990 graduation commencement speaker. Some of the seniors were hesitant about her appropriateness as a role model for the issues facing today's modern woman.

"To honor Barbara Bush as a commencement speaker," they protested, "is to honor a woman who has gained recognition through the achievements of her husband, which contradicts what we have been taught the past four years."

The first lady handled the accusations in her normal classy style and didn't allow the protests to either offend or intimidate her. Mrs. Bush spoke from her heart and the fulfillment she had experienced from her traditional values. She offered this advice in her commencement address:

"Cherish your human connections, your relationships with friends and family. For several years, you've had impressed upon you the importance to your career of dedication and hard work.

The primary joy of life is the acceptance, approval, sense of appreciation, and companionship of our human comrades. Many men do not understand that the need for fellowship is really as deep as the need for food, and so they go throughout life accepting many substitutes for genuine, warm, simple relatedness.
JOSH
LIEBMAN

"This is true, but as important as your obligations as a doctor, lawyer, or business leader will be, you are a human being first and those human connections—with spouses, with children, with friends—are the most important investments you will ever make.

"At the end of your life, you will never regret not having passed one more test, not winning one more verdict, or not closing one more deal. You will regret time not spent with a husband, a friend, a child, or a parent."

The first lady addressed the heart of living. All of our personal and professional endeavors are made sweeter, richer, and more satisfying by sharing them with others. As Antoine de Saint-Exupery wrote, "There is no joy except in human relationships."

Too often, what should matter most in our lives receives the least attention. Battles with the almighty dollar, pursuing selfish interests, attaining that next promotion, or closing a deal are empty pursuits without the human element. It's easy to overlook that our relationships are what encourage the heart and nourish the soul.

Harold Kushner, writing in *When All You've Ever Wanted Isn't Enough,* said: "A life without people, without the same people day after day, people who belong to us, people who will be there for us, people who need us and whom we need in return, may be very rich in other things, but in human terms, it is no life at all."

A life without relationships limits the value of everything you do. Regardless of the pressures you feel to succeed in our what's-in-it-for-me society, don't make the mistake of placing value on only those activities and goals that enhance your paycheck. Make time to reach out to those who add meaning to your life. And when the ties have been broken by disagreement or misunderstanding, reach out with a spirit of forgiveness.

Only you can know how much you can give to every aspect of your life. Try to decide what is the most important. And if you do, then only occasionally will you resent or regret the demands of the marriage, the career, or the child, or the staying.
BARBARA WALTERS

BE WILLING TO SAY "I'M SORRY"

*The most
deadly of all
sins is the
mutilation of a
child's spirit.*

ERIK H.
ERIKSON

After 15 years of being a parent, I think I'm finally realizing what I cherish most about my children: our relationship.

Oh, I admit it's nice when they score points in a basketball game or gracefully perform a dance routine. I'm pleased when their report cards reveal above-average performance or when I observe the sweat and effort put into a school project. And of course it's flattering when people comment how nice they look or how respectful they are.

But what really trips my trigger and renews my parental energy—after returning from a speaking trip, or working on a free-throw shot, playing taxi driver, or setting curfew—is a loving smile, a hug, a high five, and the four cherished words: "I love you, Dad."

I'm keenly aware how my actions, words, tone of voice, or nonverbals affect the loving, caring, and mutually respectful relationship we enjoy. And, I've failed at times as a father to uphold my end of the responsibility. There have been times when I crushed my children's spirit.

When my son was in the sixth grade, another dad and I agreed to coach a traveling basketball team. Along with our two sons, we invited ten other boys to enjoy the experience with us.

It didn't take long for me to realize that the definition of a father–coach is someone who expects his son to be everything he wasn't. I upheld high and sometimes unrealistic expectations. I even found it easy to justify my demands by attempting to motivate my son to be the best he could be. However, during one game I overstepped my parental privileges.

The game was already won. The boys fought courageously to overcome a major point deficit to hold a comfortable lead with 37 seconds left in the game. Out of nowhere Matt (my son) stole the ball, dribbled the length of the court, and MISSED an uncontested layup.

I chose to release my accumulated tension from the game on my son for missing that layup. The shot meant nothing. We had won the game and advanced to the finals. Matt played with heart and gave his all . . . yet he blew that simple layup. I let him know in no uncertain terms how disappointed I was and how ridiculous it was for him to miss such a simple shot.

The joy of winning drained from his face. He stood motionless and speechless as Dad continued to drain the power from his self-esteem battery. I knew I'd blown it but continued to justify my outburst and dig myself into a deeper hole.

It was a long and quiet few hours waiting for the championship game. Matt was hurting inside, and I was full of guilt. There was little question that I needed my son's forgiveness.

Sitting in our van outside the gymnasium, I slowly turned to look into Matt's fearful and discouraged face. "Matt, I was wrong," I began. "I'm sorry for blowing up at you. You worked hard in that game, and I failed to recognize you for all the good things you did. Please forgive me."

It was then Matt touched my heart and filled my eyes with tears. "It's okay, Dad. I know you love me."

Thanks to my son, I could walk into the championship game with a clear conscience, repaired heart, and softer spirit.

We lost the championship game by one point, but I came out of that tournament a winner. My son had forgiven me.

I realized in the van with Matt that day that I had admitted and he had acknowledged that I was human. Most important, Matt knew that I knew I was wrong and was willing to admit it.

The only way to heal a damaged spirit is to swallow the parental pride and say, "I'm sorry. I was wrong. Please forgive me." Failure to bring healing when you've been unfair or hurtful can breed anger for years to come.

If you were to ask what is the hardest task in the world, you might think of some muscular feat, some acrobatic challenge, some chore to be done on the battlefield or the playing field. Actually, there is nothing which we find more arduous than saying, "I was wrong."
SUNSHINE
MAGAZINE

LET GO OF THE PAST

Forgiveness is the key that unlocks the door of resentment and the handcuffs of hate. It is a power that breaks the chains of bitterness and the shackles of selfishness.
WILLIAM ARTHUR WARD

I was fairly young when the movie *The Hiding Place* was released. The impact of this dramatic story detailing one family's efforts to hide Jews in Holland from the Nazis and their later suffering in a Nazi death camp remains with me many years later. Corrie ten Boom and her family were featured in the movie, and later she returned to that death camp in Germany to deliver a message of forgiveness to a group of German people. Little did she know that this experience would test her forgiving spirit.

In her book *Tramp for the Lord,* Corrie recalls, "The place was Ravensbruck and the man who was making his way forward had been a guard—one of the most cruel guards.

"Now he was in front of me, hand thrust out: 'A fine message, Fraulein! How good it is to know that, as you say, all our sins are at the bottom of the sea!'

"And I, who had spoken so glibly of forgiveness, fumbled in my pocketbook rather than take that hand. He would not remember me, of course—how could he remember one prisoner among those thousands of women?

"But I remember him and the leather crop swinging from his belt. I was face-to-face with one of my captors and my blood seemed to freeze.

"'You mentioned Ravensbruck in your talk,' he was saying. 'I was a guard there.' No, he did not remember me.

"'But since that time,' he went on, 'I have become a Christian. I know that God has forgiven me for the cruel things I did there, but I would like to hear it from your lips as well. Fraulein'—again the hand came out—'will you forgive me?'

"And I stood there—I whose sins had again and again to be forgiven—and could not forgive. Betsie [Corrie's sister] had died in that place—could he erase her slow terrible death simply for the asking?

"It could not have been many seconds that he stood there—hand held out—but to me it seemed hours as I wrestled with the most difficult thing I had ever had to do."

Visualize that scene in your mind. Try to feel what Corrie ten Boom felt, although I doubt that any of us can come close to the inner struggle she was experiencing. How could this man expect to be forgiven for the cruel and inhumane treatment he delivered? How could he have the audacity to suggest that Corrie offer him release from his past?

Mahatma Gandhi believed that "the weak can never forgive. Forgiveness is the attribute of the strong." Corrie ten Boom was a strong person, a gallant believer in the benefits of two-way forgiveness. She forgave. I believe Corrie ten Boom not only released that prison guard from a past of regret but made a critical leap forward in her own faith, inner healing, and ability to move forward.

We all experience various ups and downs in our relationships. Some of us have been hurt by those we love the most. Others live in a daily environment of put-downs and disrespect. There are people who dread the encounter of someone who has broken their spirit and still others who shudder every time they think about people who have destroyed their trust.

Hurt people are everywhere. Relationships are in shambles. Loneliness is rampant. Undeserved unfairness, injustice, or even abandonment happens. Isolation becomes the escape for many.

There are many people out there waiting to hear the words "I forgive you," while many victims are finding a way to pay them back or seek revenge. We've become a nation obsessed with getting even. How else can you explain the headlines in our newspapers? Neighbors threatening neighbors. Lawsuits (for the most ridiculous reasons). Shootings in schools. Grudges leading to beatings. Stalkings. Parents kidnapping their own children from the other parent. The list is depressing.

Ernest Hemingway, in his short story "The Capital of the World," tells the story of a father and his teenaged son living in Spain. Through a series of events, their relationship became strained and eventually shattered. The boy opted to flee from his home, and the father began a desperate search for his lost, rebellious, yet loved son.

Running out of options, the father resorted to placing an ad in the Madrid newspaper. His son's name was Paco, a common name in Spain. The ad simply read: "Dear Paco, meet me in front of the Madrid newspaper office tomorrow at noon. All is forgiven. I love you."

Hemingway then provides us with an incredible picture and message. The next day at noon in front of the newspaper office, there were 800 "Pacos" all seeking forgiveness.

There are countless people in this world waiting to be forgiven. There are just as many who could benefit from forgiving. Show me a person who lives in peace with himself or herself and with others and I'll show you a person who freely and sincerely forgives. Forgiveness is the bridge we all must cross to leave pain, heartache, despair, anger, and hurt behind. It takes tremendous courage, humility, and a willingness to risk to cross that bridge, but on the other side peace, joy, love, and comfort await us. To fully forgive allows us to fully live.

So often people dwell on past bitterness and present themselves as a martyr for having endured. Unfortunately, the feelings of anger, mistrust, and resentment seep into their other relationships and poison what could otherwise be a healthy experience. There is only one cure and that is to forgive and let it go. Brian Tracy suggests that we "issue a blanket pardon to everyone for everything that they have ever done to hurt you in any way."

I in no way want to suggest this will be easy. In fact, Laurence Sterne said, "Only the brave know how to forgive . . . a coward never forgave; it is not in his nature." I figure if Corrie ten Boom could muster the courage to forgive the man responsible for her torment, who am I to pass eternal judgment and harbor lifelong resentment for the comparatively insignificant abuses I've experienced.

A few years ago, our high school put on the play *Joseph and the Amazing Technicolor Dreamcoat.* In addition to the enjoyment of watching my son perform on stage, I was once again reminded how this young biblical character was mistreated and hated by his brothers. Joseph was a young visionary who often had dreams about the future. What really irked his brothers is that in one dream he saw himself as ruling over his family. The brothers didn't take kindly to that. The brothers were also a bit jealous about their father's visible favoritism toward Joseph, which included the gift of a multicolored coat. Joseph's brothers figured enough is enough so they grabbed him, tossed him into a pit, and sold him into slavery.

Joseph endured the rejection of his own blood, working for a wealthy Egyptian whose wife had a thing for Joseph and continually tried to seduce him. He was wrongly accused and imprisoned. Joseph was later released, gained favor with the king, offered power and privileges second only to the king, and was ultimately highly esteemed by others.

Here's where the story gets interesting. Years after his brothers' betrayal they came to Egypt during a time of famine looking for help from the government. Little did they know their little brother Joseph was in charge of those services. Joseph immediately recognized his brothers but it was clear to Joseph that they didn't recognize him. Joseph possessed the power to get sweet revenge, but what did he do? Joseph rose above past circumstances, refused to cast blame, and responded to his brothers in love, acceptance, and forgiveness.

Letting go of the past provides a springboard for our lives to move into the future. Corrie ten Boom did it, Joseph did it, Ronald Reagan did it, and so can you.

In *Angels Don't Die,* Patti Davis shares the impact of the attitude of her father, Ronald Reagan, had on her after the 1982 assassination attempt.

Doing an injury puts you below your enemy; revenging one makes you but even with him; forgiving it sets you above him.
BENJAMIN FRANKLIN

"The following day my father said he knew his physical healing was directly dependent on his ability to forgive John Hinckley. By showing me that forgiveness is the key to everything, including physical health and healing, he gave me an example of Christ-like thinking."

ACCEPTANCE

○

If you are losing a tug-of-war with a tiger, give
him the rope before he gets to your arm. You can
always buy a new rope.

MAX GUNTHER

MY WIFE IS ALWAYS RIGHT

A message on my desk indicated that my wife had called while I was in an early-morning meeting. The note stated I was to call her as soon as possible.

Marty rarely calls me at work. She's made it a habit not to interrupt my day unless there is an emergency or an issue needing immediate attention. As a result, I was a bit anxious returning her call.

"Hello, sweetheart," I said. "What's up?"

"A bad thing happened," she sheepishly replied. "You know, it's really noisy when you back your car into the garage door."

"Pardon me," I responded while quickly attempting to visualize the scene.

"It's your fault," she continued. "When you left for work this morning, you left your garage door open. I entered the garage through your open door, and the garage was so well lit from the outside light I didn't realize my door was closed."

"It's my fault?" I chuckled.

"Yes, and now the door is shattered."

Marty and I have laughed about that situation many times, and I, of course, continue to remind her that I was not the one in the driver's seat. However, I learned a few important things about potential conflicts, arguments, and marital disputes from this unfortunate incident. First, scratched bumpers and dented trunks can be fixed. They are not worth getting upset about, especially at the expense of harmony.

Second (and this is most important), I learned that my wife is always right. Now don't get me wrong here. I don't mean to say that I am always wrong, but I carefully choose the issues worth debating. I often recall the advice of Jonathan Kozol: "Pick battles big enough to matter, small enough to win." In other words, decide what issues are worth dying for and which ones you refuse to argue about.

The newspaper and magazine editor H. L. Mencken often drew letters of criticism and outrage for his critiques of American life. He answered every critical letter and handled each one the same way. Mencken simply wrote back, "You may be right." What a marvelous way to diffuse a potentially volatile situation.

For most of us the hardest thing to give is . . . "giving in." Wanting to win fuels the fire and often causes arguments to digress into a lose–lose situation. Maybe that's why Ben Franklin believed, "If you argue and rankle and contradict, you may achieve a victory sometimes; but it will be an empty victory because you will never get your opponent's good will."

Franklin's comment reminds me of the couple traveling down the highway in complete silence. An earlier argument left both unwilling to concede their positions. Passing a barnyard of mules, the husband sarcastically asked, "Are they relatives of yours?"

"Yes," his wife replied. "I married into the family." Ouch!

Sydney J. Harris submitted, "The most important thing in an argument, next to being right, is to leave an escape hatch for your opponent, so that he can gracefully swing over to your side without too much apparent loss of face." That's why I've adopted the attitude that my wife (and other potential opponents) are always right, even though in the long run my conviction might be proven right.

What's the benefit of taking such an approach? Isn't this a chicken way out? I suppose you could look at it like that.

Even though I know there are two sides to every issue—my side and the side that no informed, intelligent, clear-thinking, self-respecting person could possibly hold (only kidding)—any quarrel will not last long if we refuse to continue stirring it up by trying to prove others wrong.

The story is told about two guys, Jake and Sam, who were stuck together on a deserted island. They got along so well that not even a cross word passed between them. In fact, their passive behavior made life so harmonious that it became monotonous at times.

One day Jake came up with an idea to break the boredom. "Let's have a heated argument," he suggested, "like people back home often have." Sam responded, "But we don't have anything to argue about." Jake thought for a moment and then suggested, "Let's find a bottle that's washed up on shore and place it on the beach between us. I'll say, 'This bottle is mine!' And you'll say, 'No, it isn't, the bottle is mine!' That will surely get a good argument started."

So, finding a bottle and placing it on the sandy beach between them, Jake exclaimed, "This bottle is mine!" Sam, pausing a moment, responded meekly, "I think, my friend, that the bottle is mine." "Oh, really," Jake said agreeably, "if the bottle is yours, take it."

It is not humanly possible to carry on an argument between two people when one refuses to argue. So, here's a thought: Let people be right until the heat has subsided and you can discuss the situation rationally.

Two months after our car crashed into the garage door and we had purchased a minivan with a luggage carrier (don't get ahead of me), I got another call at work. "Glenn, you closed your door but my garage door didn't go up high enough so the luggage carrier hooked the garage door and shattered it. The luggage carrier isn't in such good shape either."

You can draw your own conclusions on how this conversation ended.

Over the years I've come to know that there are times when it is best to simply accept my wife's point of view, especially at times when emotions can run high (like after the second garage-door mishap). I know that I can always broach the subject later and rationally discuss the situation. What almost invariably happens is that later, when we're both feeling more rational, we're not interested in who was at fault. What seemed like a major issue earlier suddenly doesn't seem so important, and what may have ended in a disagreement is now a calm discussion without mention of who's wrong or right.

A married couple were involved in another round of repeated disagreements. The same issue had been bitterly discussed over and over. The wife finally blurted in desperation, "You're impossible!"

Not missing a beat, the husband retorted, "No, I'm next to impossible."

CREATING A RELATIONSHIP
MASTERPIECE

L et's carry David Viscott's artistic thought a bit further. Consider the following qualities present in relationship masterpieces.

Start with a blank canvas of acceptance. Permit people to be who they are—not what they could be, should be, or would be if only they listened to you. Accept the imperfections and celebrate each person's individuality. Acceptance affirms people's value, raises self-esteem, and makes them feel comfortable in your presence.

Artists are masters at the use of primary colors, which create the heart of the finished product. Mutual trust is one such primary ingredient. We live in an imperfect, messy world made up of imperfect people. Unfortunately, many of us are prone to trusting people when they prove themselves trustworthy. I tend to believe that if we trust people, they will prove themselves trustworthy. I know trust can be betrayed but it is essential for relationships to develop. Step out. Make an effort to believe in the intrinsic goodness of people. Sure you might be disappointed at times, but you will also be blessed.

Share yourself with others. There is a bit of risk here but withholding who we are places a permanent blemish on the relationship canvas. Open and honest communication stands out in any close friendship. Use discretion but share your hurts, fears, and failures. Throw the good stuff in there too. Just refrain from unnecessary critical, cheap shots or hurting comments that are better left unsaid.

I'm sure every artist has his or her favorite color that tends to find its way into each creation. My favorite relationship ingredient is improving the ability to see the good in people. Tell your friends, family, and coworkers what you like about them. Tell people how thankful you are for them. Recognize their talents, applaud their successes (one of the most difficult actions of human nature), and make others feel important about themselves. Expressing appreciation on every possible occasion is one of the surest ways to boost mutual respect and encourage positive behaviors.

A masterpiece stands out in the viewer's mind when the proper highlights are added. When it comes to relationships, you can move to the next level by:

Giving more than you get

Allowing people to have their space

Maintaining confidentiality

Giving supportive and positive advice

Being loyal

Listening

Treating others with dignity

Saying "please" and "thank you"

Being agreeable

Accepting others' opinions

Forgiving wrongs committed

Quality relationships are most fulfilling. Relationships don't fail to become a beautiful experience because they are wrong but because most people don't want to invest what it takes to create an original. To evaluate how effective you are in creating a relationship masterpiece, just ask yourself, "If I were my friend, would I enjoy the artistic strokes (qualities) I experience being with me?"

LOYALTY

I'm very loyal in a
relationship.
When I go out with my mom,
I don't look at other moms.
I don't go, "Oooh, I wonder
what her macaroni and cheese
tastes like."

GARY SHANDLING

SHE COULD HAVE
MARRIED MOZART

Joe was a little shy in his teenage years, and even in college he found it difficult to ask girls out on dates. One night a buddy, Jake, who lived down the hall from Joe in the same dormitory presented an offer he couldn't refuse. "I've got great news," Jake began. "I've lined you up with a great date for Saturday night. Everything is set."

"Who is it?" Joe asked. It turned out to be a friend of Jake's girlfriend, who was going to be visiting for the weekend. Joe had never met her. "No, thank you," Joe said. "Blind dates aren't for me."

"No need to worry about this one," Jake reassured Joe. "Julie's a terrific girl. And trust me—she's a beauty."

"No," Joe repeated.

"This is a no-fail situation. I'll even give you an out."

Now he had Joe's attention. "How?" Joe asked.

"When we get to the dorm room to pick them up, wait for her to come to the door and check her out. If you like what you see, then great, we're off for a super evening. But if she's ugly, fake an asthma attack. Just go 'Aaahhhgggggg!' and grab your throat as if you're having trouble breathing. When she asks, 'What's wrong?' you say, 'It's my asthma.' And so we'll call off the date. Just like that. No questions asked. No problem."

Joe was hesitant, to say the least, but agreed to give it a try. What did he have to lose?

When they got to the door, Joe knocked and she came to the door. He took one look at her and couldn't believe his eyes. She was beautiful. How lucky could he get? He hardly knew what to say.

She took one look at Joe and went, "Aaahhhgggggg!"

It seems they weren't the only ones with a foolproof plan. Most of us, at one time or another, have been rejected by someone because we weren't smart enough, tall enough, athletic enough, good looking enough, or whatever. It's tough to feel rejected.

When we unconditionally accept someone, we give them the freedom to be on the outside who they are on the inside. True acceptance will allow us to see the real value of a human being.

The young woman who was engaged to Mozart, before he rose to fame, could have benefited from a spirit of unconditional acceptance. Impressed by more handsome men, she became disenchanted with him because he was so short. She ultimately gave him up for someone tall and attractive. When the world began to recognize Mozart for his outstanding musical accomplishments, she regretted her decision. "I knew nothing of the greatness of his genius," she said. "I only saw him as a little man."

Acceptance communicates love and value and gives people the self-confidence to become all they can be. It also allows them to be who they are until they become what they are capable of becoming.

When Marty and I were dating, I knew we were going to have a wonderful future together. If she would only make a few changes that future could be even brighter. I'm not naive, so I certainly didn't bring up the issue during our dating and refrained from talking about it on our honeymoon.

Within a few weeks of settling into marital bliss, I decided it was time to bring my suggested changes to the surface. I was bold and stupid enough to verbalize my thoughts at supper one night. I gracefully, lovingly, and rather forthrightly stated my case. Wow, did I learn a ton about marriage that night. I also gleaned a valuable lesson about acceptance.

When we attempt to force people to be who we want them to be, the defensive, stubborn, and hurt qualities emerge. However, when you allow people to refuse to change, you give them the freedom to change.

Refrain from accepting people based on what they could be, should be, or would be if only they listened to you. Until we accept unconditionally, we will continually be looking through the filters of musts, shoulds, ought-to's, have-to's, and prejudices.

Eugene Kennedy suggests that, "When someone prizes us just as we are, he or she confirms our existence." After being married over 20 years I'm realizing the value of loving someone regardless of who they are or aren't, what they have or don't have, or for what they do or don't do.

I love the *Peanuts* cartoon where Lucy says to Snoopy:

"There are times when you really bug me, but I must admit there are also times when I feel like giving you a big hug."

Snoopy replies:

"That's the way I am . . . huggable and buggable."

Seems to me that might be an appropriate description for most people in this world . . . huggable and buggable. Love them anyway.

Here's a flash of insight from *Newsweek* magazine. According to reported research, the spotted owl's greatest threat may not be logging, but one of its relatives.

For the past several years, the barred owl has been rapidly migrating westward. Barred owls, which used to live exclusively east of the Mississippi, enjoy the same food as spotted owls but are more aggressive and adaptable.

Sometimes, even our relatives (whom we can't choose) cause us the most difficulty. It's then we need a good friend who won't fight us but will participate with us in the things we both enjoy.

I HAVE A PROPOSITION
FOR YOU

In my senior year of college I took a class entitled "Marriage and the Family." I wasn't even dating anyone at the time but I figured why not prepare for future possibilities. The professor was an entertaining person and offered ample personal examples from his marriage to liven up the lecture. At the time, I questioned the validity of his stories but now that I've been married 25 years I understand how even the most outlandish ones could be true.

He began his lecture one day with this bold statement: "The secret of a successful marriage is this: Marriage is not a 50–50 proposition. A 50–50 proposition is one where nobody is giving anything.

"Rather, the secret of a happy marriage is 60–40. The husband gives in 60 percent of the time and expects his wife to give in 40 percent of the time. The wife gives in 60 percent of the time and expects her husband to give in 40 percent of the time. In a 60–40 proposition, you don't clash in the

Whoever thinks marriage is a 50–50 proposition doesn't know the half of it.

FRANKLIN P. JONES

middle and say, 'Now, it's your turn.' Instead, you intersect and overlap, because you're each giving 60 percent."

I walked out of that classroom, along with 75 other students, and never thought about the 60–40 proposition again, except of course when it appeared on the final exam. I'm not sure there is any magic formula for successful marriage, but I remain intrigued by the concept of always giving a little more than the other person. There is some truth in the saying that "marriage is an empty box. It remains empty unless you put more in than you take out."

There are no doubt a multitude of attitudes, abilities, and opinions about what makes a marriage work. In fact, I've pulled together a few tidbits of marriage wisdom. I thought you might enjoy a wide spectrum of perspectives on the joys of tying the knot. Some of the ideas reflect marvelous wisdom while others are intended to offer a bit of levity.

○

The difference between a successful marriage and a mediocre one consists of leaving about three things a day unsaid.

MICHELLE GELMAN

The failure of modern marriage is, in large measure, accounted for by our failure to employ humor in the process of marital adjustment.

JULIUS GORDON

Only two things are necessary to keep one's wife happy. First is to let her think she's having her own way. Second is to let her have it.

LADY BIRD JOHNSON

Marriage is not just spiritual communion and passionate embraces; marriage is also three-meals-a-day and remembering to carry out the trash.

DR. JOYCE BROTHERS

A happy wife sometimes has the best husband, but more often makes the best of the husband she has.

MARK BELTAIRE

It takes a loose rein to keep a marriage tight.

JOHN STEVENSON

Marriage is popular because it combines the maximum of temptation with the maximum of opportunity.

GEORGE BERNARD SHAW

Marriage resembles a pair of shears, so joined that they cannot be separated; often moving in opposite directions, yet always punishing anyone who comes between them.

SYDNEY SMITH

Marriage should be a duet—when one sings, the other claps.

JOE MURRAY

I've never thought about divorce. I've thought about murder, but never divorce.

DR. JOYCE BROTHERS

Marriage is a lot like taking vitamins. It's a process that involves the supplementation of each other's minimum daily requirements.

PAUL NEWMAN

Sometimes I wonder if men and women really suit each other. Perhaps they should live next door and just visit now and then.

KATHARINE HEPBURN

One of the reasons I made the most important decision of my life—to marry George Bush—is because he made me laugh. It's true, sometimes we laugh through our tears, but that shared laughter has been one of our strongest bonds.

BARBARA BUSH

There is no more lovely, friendly and charming relationship, communion or company than a good marriage.

MARTIN LUTHER

People are always asking couples whose marriage has endured at least a quarter of a century for their secret for success. Actually, it is no secret at all. I am a forgiving woman. Long ago, I forgave my husband for not being Paul Newman.

ERMA BOMBECK

Lots of people have asked me what Gracie and I did to make our marriage work. It's simple—we didn't do anything. I think the trouble with a lot of people is that they work too hard at staying married. They make a business out of it. When you work too hard at a business, you get tired; and when you get tired, you get grouchy; and when you get grouchy, you start fighting; and when you start fighting, you're out of business.

GEORGE BURNS

An archaeologist is the best husband any woman can have.
The older she gets, the more he is interested in her!

AGATHA CHRISTIE

Some people ask the secret of our long marriage. We take
time to go to a restaurant two times a week. A little
candlelight, dinner, soft music and dancing. She goes
Tuesdays. I go Fridays.

HENNY YOUNGMAN

We have a picture of the perfect partner, but we marry an
imperfect person. Then we have two options. Tear up the
picture and accept the person, or tear up the person and
accept the picture.

J. GRANT HOWARD, JR.

It destroys one's nerves to be amiable every day to the same
human being.

BENJAMIN DISRAELI

Familiarity breeds contempt—and children.

MARK TWAIN

The most important thing a father can do for his children is to love their mother.

REV. THEODORE HESBURGH

More marriages might survive if the partners realized that sometimes the better comes after the worse.

DOUG LARSON

After winning an argument with his wife, the wisest thing a man can do is apologize.

ANN LANDERS

We sleep in separate rooms; we have dinner apart; we take separate vacations—we're doing everything we can to keep our marriage together.

RODNEY DANGERFIELD

And finally from the 1763 King of Poland, Stanislaus Leszcynski:

In marrying, you vow to love one another. Would it not be better for your happiness if you vowed to please one another.

UNDERSTANDING

○

*If I can listen to what he tells me, if I can
understand how it seems to him, if I can sense
the emotional flavor which it has for him, then I
will be releasing potent forces of change within him.*

CARL ROGERS

WHOSE LANGUAGE ARE YOU SPEAKING?

D r. Robert Schuller, in his book *Reach Out for New Life,* tells a story about an incident that occurred many years ago in England. The character at the heart of the story was the most famous elephant in the circus world named Bozo.

Bozo was a beautiful beast—a great big tender hunk of gentleness. Children would come to the circus and extend their open palms, filled with peanuts, through the gate. The elephant would extend his trunk to pick the peanuts out of their hands and then curl his trunk and feed himself. He seemed to smile as he swallowed the gifts. Everyone loved Bozo.

Then one day something happened that changed his personality from positive to negative almost overnight. He almost stampeded, threatening to crush the man who was cleaning his cage. Then he began to charge the children. The circus owner knew the elephant was now dangerous and that the problem had to be faced. He came to the conclusion that he would have to exterminate this big old beast. This decision hurt him, first, because he loved the elephant; second, because it was the only elephant he had. Bozo had been imported from India, and it would cost him thousands of dollars to replace him.

Then he had an idea. This desperate and crude man decided that he would sell tickets to view the execution of Bozo. At least he would be able to raise the money to replace him.

The story spread, tickets were sold out, and the place was jammed. There, on the appointed date, was Bozo in his cage, as three men with high-powered rifles rose to take aim at the great beast's head.

Just before the signal to shoot, a little stubby man with a brown derby hat stepped out of the crowd, walked over to the owner, and said, "Sir, this is not necessary. This is not a bad elephant." The owner said, "But it is. We must kill him before he kills someone." The little man with the derby hat said, "Sir, give me two minutes alone in his cage, and I'll prove that you are wrong. He is not a bad elephant."

The circus owner thought for a moment, wrung his hands and said, "All right. But first you must sign a note absolving me of all responsibility if you get killed."

The little man scribbled on a piece of paper the words "I absolve you of all guilt," signed his name, folded the paper, and handed it to the circus owner. The owner opened the door to the cage. The little man threw his brown derby hat on the ground and stepped into the cage. As soon as he was inside, the door was locked behind him. The elephant raised his trunk and bellowed and trumpeted loudly.

But before the elephant could charge, the little man began talking to him, looking him straight in the eye. The people close by could hear the little man talking, but they couldn't understand what he was saying. It seemed as if he were speaking in an unknown tongue. The elephant still trembled, but hearing these strange words from this little man he began to whine, cry, and wave his head back and forth. The stranger walked up to Bozo and began to stroke his trunk. The now gentle beast tenderly wrapped his trunk around the feet of the little man, lifted him up, carried him around his cage, and cautiously put him back down at the door. Everyone applauded.

As he walked out of the cage, the little man said to the keeper, "You see? He is a good elephant. His only problem is that he is an Indian elephant, and he only understands

Hindustani. He was homesick for someone who could understand him. I suggest, sir, that you find someone in London who speaks Hindustani and have him come in and just talk to the elephant. You'll have no problems."

As the man picked up his derby and walked away, the circus owner looked at the note and read the signature of the man who had signed it. The man with the little brown derby was Rudyard Kipling.

Dr. Schuller said, "People also become frustrated, angry, and defeated when no one understands them." Could it be the person you are having a difficult time with just needs someone to understand their situation, to speak their language.

John Luther believed, "Natural talent, intelligence, a wonderful education—none of these guarantees success. Something else is needed: The sensitivity to understand what other people want and the willingness to give it to them."

PEOPLE DO THINGS
FOR THEIR REASONS

I think Mark Twain must have had a bad day when this quote was recorded. Although there is good reason for the common theory that a dog is man's best friend, even a dog can become disillusioned if the relationship is a one-way affair. Let me explain what I mean.

Ralph Waldo Emerson was a great historian, poet, and philosopher, but he didn't know much about getting a stubborn calf through a barn door. One day, Emerson and his son were involved in such a challenge. Can't you just see the son with his arms around the calf's neck and Emerson in the rear braced to push with all his might? As they pushed and pulled repeatedly, the calf braced itself by locking her knees and digging her feet into the ground determined not to comply.

Drenched with sweat, full of bovine smell, and frustrated to the point of exasperation, Emerson stood helpless over the calf. An Irish servant girl who had observed

If you pick up a starving dog and make him prosperous, he will not bite you. This is the principal difference between a man and a dog.
MARK TWAIN

the comical pursuit approached Emerson and asked if she could be of assistance. She walked around to the front of the calf and thrust her finger in the calf's mouth, and the calf peacefully followed the girl into the barn.

Bob Conklin, in *How to Get People to Do Things,* said, "People are like that calf. You can poke them, prod them, push them, and they don't move. But give them a good reason— one of their reasons—a way in which they will benefit, and they will follow gently along. People will do things for *their* reasons. Not *your* reasons. And those reasons are emotional, aroused by the way they feel."

People do things for their reasons, not your reasons. This is one of the greatest and yet simplest principles of human relations. People do things because they want to, not because you want them to. As Lord Chesterfield advised, "If you will please people, you must please them in their own way."

Once we understand that relationships evolve around people's needs and expectations, it's more natural to create an environment where mutual warmth and love exist.

What do people need? What are the reasons people do things? What are the qualities we display that cause people to want to pursue and maintain a relationship with us?

Don't make this too philosophical or difficult. In many ways, Anthony Robbins's comment that "When people are like each other, they tend to like each other" provides us a hint to the answers we're looking for. The same things that cause you to be drawn to someone oftentimes open the door for others to feel comfortable with you.

Make a list of the qualities, actions, and attitudes of people you enjoy being around. Endeavor to sharpen and refine those attributes in your life. There is no shortcut to nourishing relationships, but understanding what people need is the shortest way between where you are and where you want your relationships to be.

To counter Mark Twain's cynical comparison between people and dogs, perhaps we should consider that oftentimes we give more thought and energy to what our dog wants and likes than we do to our spouse, children, and friends.

Needing someone is like needing a parachute. If he isn't there the first time you need him, chances are you won't be needing him again.

DILBERT'S WORDS OF WISDOM

COULD YOU
JUST LISTEN?

Most of the successful people I've known are ones who do more listening than talking. If you choose your company carefully, it's worth listening to what they have to say. You don't have to blow out the other fellow's light to let your own shine.

BERNARD M. BARUCH

It happens about once a week. My wife and I have a nice conversation about a favorite topic, or she will fill me in on the details of an upcoming event. A little while later I ask a question that she already addressed in our conversation. Marty then looks at me and says, "You never listen to me." Ouch. I do listen, I think, but for some reason a portion of the information just seems to leak from my memory. Although I think I know how to listen, my actions often prove otherwise.

John Maxwell tells a delightful story about an 89-year-old woman with hearing problems. She visited her doctor, and after examining her, he said, "We now have a procedure that can correct your hearing problem. When would you like to schedule the operation?"

"There won't be any operation because I don't want my hearing corrected," said the woman. "I'm 89 years old, and I've heard enough!"

There are times, at any age, where we might think "I've heard enough and don't care to listen anymore." Karl

Menninger believes, "The friends who listen to us are the ones we move toward, and we want to sit in their radius." If a relationship is important to us, it's wise to remember that the difference between someone feeling comfortable with us or avoiding us often depends on our willingness to listen.

The following poem reveals the feelings of someone who badly wants to be heard.

> When I ask you to listen to me
> and you start giving me advice,
> you have not done what I asked.
>
> When I ask you to listen to me
> and you tell me I shouldn't feel that way,
> you are trampling on my feelings.
>
> When I ask you to listen to me
> and you try to solve my problems for me,
> you have failed me.
>
> Listen! All I asked was that you listen,
> not talk to or do—
> just hear me.
>
> Advice is cheap;
> the price of a newspaper will get you both
> Dear Abby and Billy Graham.

I can do for myself; I'm not helpless—
maybe discouraged and faltering
but not helpless.

So please listen and just hear me.

And if you want to talk,
wait a minute for your turn—
and I'll listen to you.

AUTHOR UNKNOWN

This unknown writer was expressing a frustration experienced by a multitude of people everyday. From the corporate office to the school playground, from the hospital room to the bedroom, and from the subway to the carpool you will find people who genuinely feel no one is interested in their life. Paul Tournier addressed this universal need. "It is impossible," he said, "to overemphasize the immense need humans have to be really listened to, to be taken seriously, to be understood. No one can develop freely in this world and find their life full, without feeling understood by at least one person. . . Listen to all the conversations of our world, between nations as well as between couples. They are for the most part, dialogues of the deaf."

Studies indicate that we spend 30 percent of a normal business day speaking, 16 percent reading, 9 percent writing, and 45 percent, the majority of our time, listening. Yet, very few people have studied or mastered listening techniques even though close to half of our day is spent in such activity.

An unofficial listening study offers this perspective: "We hear half of what is being said, listen to half of what we hear, understand half of it, believe half of that and remember only half of that." If you translate those assumptions into an eight-hour workday, it means that:

You spend about four hours in listening activities;

You hear about two hours' worth;

You actually listen to an hour's worth;

You understand 30 minutes of that hour;

You believe only 15 minutes' worth; and

You remember just under 8 minutes' worth.

Listening is primarily an activity of the mind, not the ear. When the mind is not actively involved in the process, it should be called hearing, not listening.
MORTIMER ADLER

Statistics indicate the importance and difficulty of listening as well as the widespread listening incompetence most people display. The world needs people who aspire to be listeners. Ironically, they not only enhance others' lives but their own as well. It is a win–win affair. And, the benefits of acquiring this important skill are enjoyed throughout our lives.

PLEASE UNDERSTAND ME

A few weeks into my daughter's freshman year of high school, she became frustrated. Although a normally happy, vivacious young lady, the pressures of school, conflict with friends, teacher expectations, and the time demands of extracurricular activities were a bit over- whelming. As Katy shared her traumatic experiences with me, I tried to console her by telling her everything would be okay and that she need not be distressed by these minor difficulties.

"That's easy for you to say, Dad," she responded. "You have all your problems over with."

From a teenager's perspective adults are all through with their problems and life is one continuous party. Even more important, I think Katy was trying to tell me she could use a little empathy. She wanted me to understand what it feels like to be a freshman. I gave my daughter sound, practical, and realistic advice when all she really wanted was an understanding heart. This could have been a magical father–daughter moment. Instead, it was just another conversation.

To love you as I love myself is to seek to hear you as I want to be heard and understand you as I long to be understood.
DAVID AUGSBURGER

Poet Shel Silverstein wrote a heart-touching verse entitled "The Little Boy and the Old Man." In it he portrays a young boy talking to an elderly gentleman.

The boy says, "Sometimes I drop my spoon." "I do that too," replies the old man.

"I often cry," continues the boy. The old man nods, "So do I."

"But worst of all," says the boy, "it seems grownups don't pay attention to me." Just then the boy feels "the warmth of a wrinkled hand." "I know what you mean," says the little old man.

Most people think they see the world as it is. Unfortunately, we really see the world as we are.

I saw my daughter's difficulties through the eyes of a grownup, not a high school freshman. The little boy saw the world through his eyes, which he learned were much like the eyes of the old man. In a world obsessed with "me" there is a tremendous opportunity to touch people's lives by focusing on what's important to them.

John Powell wrote, "Sometimes I think that the main obstacle to empathy is our persistent belief that everybody is exactly like us." I know that doesn't sound too profound but the significance of that statement is an entryway to people's hearts. To realize others don't necessarily think like me, act like me, feel as I feel, or respond to every situation as I would respond prepares me to gain valuable insights that might otherwise have been overlooked.

The ability to truly understand other people is a valuable asset. It involves opening your mind and heart with an insatiable desire to help people feel understood. A sincere attempt is made in every conversation to think how others think and feel what others are feeling. If every conversation began and evolved around this intent, I wonder how many conflicts could be avoided.

Are your daily conversations motivated by a desire to get people to understand you, or are you committed in every conversation to put yourself in the other person's world? See her world, experiences, hopes, fears, and dreams as she sees them. The benefits are immeasurable because for every person we sincerely seek to understand, there will be someone who wants to do the same for us.

Make it possible for someone today to say, "When I'm with you, I feel understood."

Sometimes you can defuse a difficult situation simply by being willing to understand the other person. Often all that people need is to know that someone else cares about how they feel and is attempting to understand their position.
BRIAN TRACY

⬡

ENCOURAGEMENT

You can't make the other fellow feel
important in your presence if you secretly
feel that he is a nobody.

LES GIBLIN

HOW GOOD CAN
PEOPLE BE?

I read about a young football coach at Louisiana State University who knew how to capitalize on high expectations. Paul Dietzel's 1958 football team was picked to finish near the bottom of the Southeastern Conference. Of his top 30 players, none of them weighed over 210 pounds and their abilities were far from impressive. Dietzel eliminated the customary first-, second-, and third-team concept and, instead, broke his squad into three units and named them the White Team, Go Team, and Chinese Bandits. The Chinese Bandit squad would customarily be known as benchwarmers. However, Dietzel convinced them they were defensive specialists and challenged them to live up to their name.

Throughout the season, the Chinese Bandits were called upon to display their tough and aggressive defensive tactics that frequently spelled the difference between winning and losing. That year, L.S.U. defied all odds by going undefeated

The only person who behaves sensibly is my tailor. He takes new measurements every time he sees me. All the rest go on with their old measurements.
GEORGE BERNARD SHAW

and being named the number-one team in both the Associated Press and United Press polls.

The 1958 L.S.U. football team wasn't technically very good, but Dietzel never let them know it. He wasn't like the football coach who told his team, "We are undefeated and untied. Nobody has scored on us. Enjoy it because we now have to play our first game." Dietzel instilled a belief in his players that they could succeed and that belief produced the power to live up to his expectations.

How good would you be if you didn't know how good you were? How good would your team be if they didn't know how good they were? How good could those around you become if you raised your expectations of them?

Create high expectations for people and let them know you believe in them more than they believe in themselves. People succeed if someone they respect thinks they can.

OFFER A SHOULDER
TO LEAN ON

The 1992 Olympics in Barcelona, Spain provided spectators with a multitude of great moments. Reruns of one track-and-field event live in my memory.

Britain's Derek Redmond had a lifelong dream of winning a gold medal in the 400-meter race. His chances of achieving that dream increased when the gun sounded to begin the semifinals in Barcelona. Redmond was running a great race, and the finish line was clearly in sight as he rounded the turn in the backstretch. Then disaster struck. A sharp pain shot up the back of his leg. He fell face-first onto the track with a torn right hamstring.

Sports Illustrated provided this account of the events that followed:

As the medical attendants were approaching, Redmond fought to his feet. "It was animal instinct," he would say later. He set out hopping, in a crazed attempt to finish the race.

Few things in the world are more powerful than a positive push. A smile. A word of optimism and hope. A 'you can do it' when things are tough.

RICHARD M. DEVOS

When he reached the stretch, a large man in a T-shirt came out of the stands, hurled aside a security guard and ran to Redmond, embracing him. It was Jim Redmond, Derek's father. "You don't have to do this," he told his weeping son. "Yes, I do," said Derek. "Well, then," said Jim, "we're going to finish this together."

And they did. Fighting off security men, the son's head sometimes buried in his father's shoulder, they stayed in Derek's lane all the way to the end, as the crowd gaped, then rose and howled and wept.

What a dramatic sight! Derek Redmond failed to capture a gold medal, but he left Barcelona with an incredible memory of a father who left the crowd to share his son's pain. Together, they limped to the finish.

There isn't a person alive who hasn't experienced the disappointment of unmet expectations. Things don't always go as planned in the pursuit of our dreams. Unexpected obstacles, unplanned events, or the onset of circumstances beyond our control can burst our bubble. It is amazing how quickly our hopes can vanish followed by the pangs of failure, embarrassment, and discouragement.

A word of encouragement during a failure is worth more than a whole load of praise after a success. Orison Swett

Marden said, "There is no medicine like hope, no incentive so great, and no tonics so powerful as expectation of something better tomorrow." You can be the distributor of hope that propels someone past the present burden and into future possibilities.

    Understanding how quickly momentum can be brought to an abrupt halt increases our sensitivity to how others feel when disappointments sabotage their dreams. It's then that people need someone who cares enough about them to come out of the crowd and on to the track. Let them know you are there for them. Offer a shoulder to lean on to help carry them through the pain. They may not attain the level of success they aspired to, but they'll never forget the person who lifted them up when they felt let down.

The worst part of success is trying to find someone who is happy for you.
BETTE MIDLER

HELP PEOPLE BELIEVE
IN THEMSELVES

*Those who
believe in our
ability do more
than stimulate
us. They create
for us an
atmosphere in
which it
becomes easier
to succeed.*

JOHN H.
SPALDING

Yogi Berra was asked whether he thought Don Mattingly's performance in 1984 exceeded his expectations. Yogi responded, "No, but he did a lot better than I thought he would."

Yogi Berra is a master of confusing messages. Yet, our message concerning what we expect of others is normally received loud and clear.

Tommy was having a difficult time in school. He was full of questions and tended to fall behind on class assignments. Tommy's teacher became frustrated with his performance and told his mother Tommy had little chance for academic achievement or life success.

Tommy's mother believed differently. She removed Tommy from the low-expectation environment and taught him herself. She nurtured his inquisitive nature and encouraged him to use failure as a signal to find another way.

Tommy did all right for himself. He became an inventor, recording more than a thousand patents. We can thank him for the lights in our homes and countless other electronic inventions. Thomas Edison thrived on the hope created by his mother's positive expectations.

Our mission in relationships should not be to impress others but to get people to believe in themselves. When we express faith, the door is opened for people to think higher of themselves. That confidence in themselves creates an environment in which people feel safe to risk going beyond where they are. Every time you express positive expectations in someone, you're providing life-sustaining nutrition.

Rent the movie *Stand and Deliver*. Watch how calculus teacher Jaime Escalante works with high-school students in East Los Angeles. Keep in mind this is a part of the country where high expectations are virtually nonexistent, and the idea of quality education is a hopeless pursuit.

Escalante endeavors to work with his students to exceed all previous societal and self-imposed limitations. He's committed to offering them an opportunity to believe in themselves and create hope for the future. The kids respond.

Keep away from people who try to belittle your ambitions. Small people always do that, but the really great make you feel that you, too, can become great.

MARK TWAIN

I smiled when the Educational Testing Service voiced their skepticism about the results earned by Escalante's students. The ETS investigates the class for cheating. Ultimately, the service provider had to admit that Escalante's students had honorably achieved their scores. This great teacher challenged their minds and instilled a belief in themselves.

In order for us to get people to feel important, we must see their value. What we look for in people, we can see. What we see, we communicate. What we communicate stimulates people to respond accordingly. What do you see in and expect of others?

REDUCING THE STING
OF CRITICISM

F ace it, some people have photographic memories. They remember all the negatives about the people around them. You have probably encountered such a person somewhere in your life and have scrambled to avoid his or her crushing blows. Although it's true that criticism won't kill you, its sting can have a lasting impact.

It's difficult to live out the wisdom of Charles Spurgeon, who said, "Insults are like bad coins; we cannot help their being offered to us, but we need not take them." Easier said than done. Criticism seems to immediately cut its way to our emotional center and leave undesirable scars.

We do have a choice in how we deal with the insults we encounter, and we must realize that no matter how small or large the issue might be, it can be made worse or better by our reaction. When I am criticized, I have a tendency to overreact and become defensive. I dwell on the comment, running it through my mind over and over attempting to justify my actions or prove mentally how wrong the other

A successful man is one who can lay a firm foundation with the bricks that others throw at him.
DAVID
BRINKLEY

person was. Incredible energy is wasted in this spiraling, unproductive activity.

The next time you find yourself in the path of critical bricks hurled your way, learn to desensitize the impact of accusations rather than stand defenseless.

1. Consider the Source. Normally it is the person who can't dance who complains about the unevenness of the floor. Likewise, people who criticize other people are frequently hurting themselves. Out of their frustration with life, they find someone else to blame. Don't take their criticism personally.

While driving along a desolate highway on a hot summer afternoon, I noticed vultures soaring high overhead, swooping down, then rising up again. Their motives were undoubtedly selfish as I watched a small group of them tear apart and devour the remains of a small animal on the side of the road. That's their lifestyle—continually on the lookout for some creature they can take advantage of. Much like the vultures, critical people tend to look for unsuspecting, vulnerable victims they can tear apart and devour. Consider the source before deciding to take seriously what has been said.

2. Smile. Have you ever tried arguing with someone who is smiling at you? If you want to disarm an attacker, take a deep breath, smile, and say, "Thank you." O. A. Bautista says, "One of the surest marks of good character is a person's ability to accept criticism without malice to the one who gives it." I might add that it takes an equally strong character to neutralize criticism before it damages yourself or the relationship. I'm not suggesting that this is easy, but you will find it helpful in keeping critical comments in perspective.

Along with your smile, keep your sense of humor intact. Humor is a marvelous tool for neutralizing the sting of criticism and disapproval. It will divert your attention and diminish the effects.

I love the story of the lady who took her overworked husband to the family physician for a checkup. The physician took the wife aside and whispered: "I don't like the way your husband looks."

"I don't either," she replied, "but he's always been a good provider."

3. *Expect It but Don't Accept It.* Epictetus provided us an ideal approach to dealing with all those people with photographic memories. "If someone criticizes you, agree at once. Mention that if only the other person knew you well, there would be more to criticize than that." Arguing with one who criticizes is a no-win battle, so Epictetus believed the

best way to silence your critics and not waste energy is to agree with them and get on with life.

Someone once said that there are only two critical people in the whole world . . . they just move around a lot and seem to pull down the masses with their criticism. "Nothing takes a greater toll on us than to be around a pessimist—a person always finding fault and criticizing others," said Cavett Robert. "We've all seen the type. He has mental B.O. He's a one-man grievance committee, always in session." Actually, criticism has become a national pastime and sooner or later you will be the target of someone's mental B.O. Not everything everybody says about you is true. It is important that you immediately and objectively weigh the value of the other's comment. Learn what you can from the criticism. If the person is right, make changes. If he or she is wrong, don't spend another moment focused on the accusations.

4. Don't Take It Personally. Abraham Lincoln would never have achieved all he did had he not learned to duck or build on the massive criticism he encountered. His insight is worth your consideration: "If I were to try to read, much less to answer, all the attacks made on me, this shop might as well be closed for any other business," Lincoln said. "I do the very best I know how—the very best I can; and I mean to keep doing so until the end. If the end brings me out all right, then what is said against me won't matter. If the end brings me out wrong, then ten angels swearing I was right would make no difference."

Colonel George Washington Goethals faced enormous opposition as the supervisor responsible for building the Panama Canal. Not only did his builders face incredible challenges with geography, climate, and disease, but people back home predicted they would never complete the "impossible task." The great engineer kept the faith and was resolute in steadily moving forward to complete the project without responding to his opposition.

At one point a frustrated coworker asked, "Aren't you going to answer your critics?" "In time," Goethals replied. "How?" the man asked. The colonel smiled and said, "With the canal!" That answer materialized on August 15, 1914, when the canal opened to traffic for the first time.

Pressing forward. Not getting caught up in verbal warfare. Producing results. Those are often the best ways to counteract ridicule. Expect it. Don't accept it. Press on.

5. *Ponder the Benefits.* When the legendary Knute Rockne was head football coach at Notre Dame, a column appeared in the school paper with no indication as to who wrote it, other than the signature "Old Bearskin." The columnist picked apart

each player, pointing out his individual weaknesses and lambasting his shortcomings and inept performance.

Word spread quickly across campus, and players complained to Rockne that they were being unfairly criticized. Rockne would empathize with their position and encourage them to get out on the field and prove their critic wrong.

The writer of that column was never identified—that is, until after Rockne died. And guess what? "Old Bearskin" was actually the players' best friend and their coach. Yes, Rockne penned the article. He was aware of what happened to football legends whose success on the field went to their heads. As "Old Bearskin," his criticisms were an attempt to help them avoid the pitfalls of pride and strive continually to achieve new levels of performance.

As unfair as criticism might be, it can also be a helpful guardian against the snares of success. Corrie ten Boom believes, "Our critics are the unpaid guardians of our souls." That may be a bit difficult to swallow, but with an open mind the perceptions of others can actually assist us in keeping our talents fine-tuned. The master retailer Marshall Field maintained a healthy attitude about criticism. He said, "Those who enter to buy, support me. Those who come to flatter, please me. Those who complain, teach me how I may please others so that more will come. Only those hurt me who are displeased but do not complain. They refuse me permission to correct my errors and thus improve my service."

I had the unfortunate experience of going to the doctor to determine the source of severe stomach pain. As I lay on the examination table he began to poke, prod, and push in various areas, all the while asking, "Does this hurt? How about this?" It was an unpleasant experience.

When I flinched with pain each time he pressed a certain area, it was evident that he was either pressing too hard, without the right sensitivity, or it was a problem area. In my case, additional tests were required resulting in the diagnosis of an infection and the need for treatment.

So it is with criticism. When you cry out with discomfort, that might be an indication there is need for additional attention. Maybe someone is just pushing a hot button and is not so sensitive as he or she should be. You can't control the critical people in your life. But what you do with criticism is your decision. And you can control the way in which you dish out criticism. Do you do it with kindness and use it to encourage others, or do you wield it as a weapon of destruction? The next time you have criticism of another that you feel you should give, be sure that the ultimate message is one of encouragement.

I can please only one person per day. Today is not your day. Tomorrow isn't looking good either.
DILBERT'S
WORDS OF
WISDOM

COMMUNICATION

○

The reason you don't understand me is because
I'm talkin' to you in English and
you're listenin' in dingbat.

ARCHIE BUNKER

FOR MEN ONLY

D r. Paul Faulkner believes there is a distinct difference in the listening ability between men and women. In his book *Making Things Right,* Dr. Faulkner suggests that women are wired for 440 volts! They have little emotional wires sticking out from them in all directions. They are wired for sound and two-way communication. They talk and receive. They hook into another person's emotions and needs.

On the other hand, men are wired for 12 volts. That's all. We have two little wires sticking out, and they're both bent. Our speakers are usually hooked up, but our receivers are dead. So we have to work a lot harder to listen than the women do. We're just wired differently. We men are like two tin cans and a waxed string. But the women are hooked up like Ma Bell.

Archie and Edith Bunker's communication difficulties probably had little to do with one speaking English and other

Before a marriage, a man will lie awake all night thinking about something you said; after marriage, he'll fall asleep before you finish saying it.

HELEN ROWLAND

communicating in "dingbat." Dr. Faulkner might suggest that Archie Bunker give some serious attention to his bent wires and dead receiver.

Now that I think about it, I'm going to put additional effort into my own 12-volt wiring system to improve my reception. What about you?

MASTER A RARE SECRET
TO SUCCESS

enry Ford suggested, "If there is any one secret to success it lies in the ability to get the other person's point of view and see things from his angle as well as your own." Effective listening plays a major role in our ability to understand situations from another person's perspective, thereby ensuring a mutual understanding. Henry Ford considered this ability so important that he promoted it as a secret to success. Consider these four major principles for successful listening. These practical and proven techniques will increase your impact on people dramatically.

You ain't learnin' nothin' when you're talkin.'
LYNDON B. JOHNSON

1. Develop a Willingness to Listen. Your heart, not your ears, determines your listening efficiency. It has been said that "when the heart is willing it will find a thousand ways, but when the heart is weak it will find a thousand excuses."

A man approached his farmer neighbor one day asking to borrow his rope. "Can't do it," the farmer replied, "I'm using it to tie up my milk."

"You can't tie up your milk with a rope," the borrower responded.

"I know," the farmer replied, "but when you don't want to do something, one excuse is as good as another."

How true! Listening is a desire, an attitude that wants to hear what others are saying. Dick Cavett explained why this attitude is so important. He said, "It's a rare person who wants to hear what he doesn't want to hear." Developing an attitude or wanting to hear is an inside job. You can read all the books, take an array of classes, or indulge yourself with other learning sources but the prerequisite to becoming an effective leader is developing a willingness to listen.

2. Be Open-Minded. "Real communication," wrote Carl Rogers, "takes place when we listen with understanding; that is, see the speaker's idea from his or her viewpoint, sense how they feel about it, and realize why they're talking about it." People can be distracted from achieving this level of communication when they jump to conclusions, find fault with the message, react to emotionally charged words, or allow their prejudices to interfere with what is being said.

I rarely travel in my car without the entertainment of a motivational or educational cassette message playing. Rarely do I argue, interrupt, or yell at my cassette player. Instead, I carefully listen to the speaker's entire message, take a few written notes, and then reflect on what has been said. In other words, even though I might not agree with everything I hear, it is not an option to listen selectively, pay attention only to what I agree with, or block out topics that fail to be appealing. It's critical to hear the whole message without making assumptions that block our ability to understand the other person's perspective.

The word "communication" comes from the Latin root which means "to have in common." When you listen, be open-minded enough to look for common ground. This open-minded approach to listening will increase your comprehension and ability to understand the ideas and feelings being shared.

I fear that far too often our listening minds are like the seasoned consultant. An aspiring management consultant was learning the ropes from an experienced senior partner. As the novice shadowed his model, he noticed how several times a day people would dump their problems on the other man. The experienced consultant would maintain eye contact, nod, and smile warmly. Then it was on to another department where the same scenario would be repeated. Day in and day out the seasoned consultant seemed to patiently listen to everyone's moans and groans.

Finally, the young man could restrain himself no longer. "I don't see how you can do it. How do you put up with listening to everyone's problems all of the time and still remain so positive?"

The older consultant flashed a wry smile and said, "Who listens?"

3. Be Attentive. President Abraham Lincoln said, "When I'm getting ready to reason with a man, I spend one third of my time thinking about myself and what I am going to say— and two thirds thinking about him and what he is going to say." Lincoln, the master communicator, knew how important it was to be attentive to those he was communicating with.

Attentive listening is difficult partly because the normal person can listen at 400–600 words per minute, while the average speaking rate is 200–300 words per minute. That leaves a substantial amount of time for the mind to wander.

Maybe this explains why the normal listener retains only 50 percent of what he or she hears; after 48 hours, retains only 25 percent; and after one week, 10 percent.

In addition, we listen at about a 25 percent efficiency rate. That means that we ignore, misunderstand, or distort a majority of what we hear.

So, how can we increase our attention quotient? Become a sponge. Soak in everything the other person is saying. Soak it up. Everything. Shut out all distractions. Remember, your mind is working at 400–600 words a minute. Therefore, to give someone your undivided attention and soak up the entire message:

Maintain comfortable eye contact. Don't stare.

Don't jump to conclusions and guess what the person is going to say next.

Refrain from interrupting. Let the person finish.

Be patient.

Listen for the spoken and unspoken message.

Don't tune people out. Keep an open mind.

Be silent. Juggle the letters in listen and "silent" emerges.

Take a few notes.

Wait to prepare your reply until the person has finished.

Nod, smile, agree with what is being said, lean slightly forward. Actively participate in the conversation.

Ask questions to clarify.

Don't allow how people say something to distract you from what they say.

Paraphrase what's been said. Make sure you have an accurate picture of the message.

These strategies take tremendous discipline and self-control. You can do it. Commit yourself and avoid the temptation to be distracted. You will pay people the utmost compliment by giving them your undivided attention.

4. Make People Glad That They Talk to You. So often I assume people talk to me because they are looking for advice. More often than not, advice is the last thing they seek. People want a sympathetic ear, one that will sincerely attempt to experience what they are feeling and accept them for it. "After 36 years," said Ann Landers, "I realize that many people who write to me don't want advice. They just need someone who will listen."

A particularly heart-warming story concerning the value of listening involves a young woman asked out on two dates. The first night she went to dinner with William E. Gladstone, the distinguished British diplomat. Upon arriving home, she was asked her opinion of the evening. "Oh," she responded, "William Gladstone is the cleverest man in England."

When her evening with the equally distinguished Benjamin Disraeli was over, the same question was posed to her. She replied thoughtfully, "Benjamin Disraeli made me feel like the cleverest woman in England."

What was the difference? It has been said that listening to someone is the highest form of compliment you can pay. That person will feel valued by your attention to them and what they have to say. Disraeli was known for his listening skills and it only followed that an evening spent with him would make anyone feel important.

George and Nikki Kochler mirror the importance of affirming people through listening: "When you and I listen to another person we are conveying the thought that 'I'm interested in you as a person, and I think that what you feel is important. I respect your thoughts, even if I don't agree with them. I know that they are valid for you. I feel sure that you have a contribution to make. I'm not trying to change you or evaluate you. I just want to understand you. I think you're worth listening to, and I want you to know that I'm the kind of person that you can talk to.'"

Is that the attitude that permeates your conversations? A credible way to evaluate that question is to answer this one: How important do people feel after spending time with me?

One often reads about the art of conversation— how it's dying or what's needed to make it flourish, or how rare good ones are. But wouldn't you agree that the infinitely more valuable rara avis *is a good listener?*
MALCOLM FORBES

UNTANGLE YOUR HORNS

I am told that displayed in an old monastery near Babenhausen, Germany are two pairs of deer antlers permanently interlocked. Apparently they were found in that position many years ago. Legend has it the animals had been fighting fiercely, and their horns became so entangled they were unable to free themselves. As a result, both deer perished from hunger.

Imagine those entangled horns. They represent the frozen condition conflict can create. When we are determined to have our own way, win every argument, or demand our rights, we risk becoming entangled to the degree that we starve a relationship. Unresolved conflict threatens to dissolve relationships.

Heightened negative emotions can also spread to those outside the initial conflict. That's what happened in the spring of 1894 when the Baltimore Orioles arrived in Boston to play a regular season, a routine baseball game. The game became anything but routine when a clash occurred between two players.

The Orioles' John McGraw got into a fight with the Boston third baseman. Within minutes both benches emptied to join the brawl. People in the grandstands decided to get involved and the conflict between fans erupted. Someone set fire to the stands, and eventually the entire ballpark burned to the ground. To make matters worse, the fire spread to 107 other Boston buildings. This unnecessary conflict turned into a community disaster.

Conflicts are inevitable, but such devastating effects can be avoided. We bring different backgrounds, experiences, opinions, and emotions into our relationships. Whenever two people interact on an ongoing basis there is bound to be some discord. Having conflict need not be perceived as abnormal. The real issue is whether or not we get it resolved.

Past experiences certainly affect our present approaches to conflict. When I was growing up my two brothers and I would periodically get into a wing-ding of an argument. My mother would immediately intercede, separate us, and tell us each to go to our rooms until we could learn to get along. But think about that a minute. It is impossible to learn how to get along with people when you are separated from them. At any rate, when I encounter conflict today, my first reaction is to go to my room (or someplace else where I can be alone).

Unfortunately, when I come out of my room the conflict is still waiting for me.

There's no magic solution for resolving conflict. There are, however, a number of actions we can take to diffuse tense situations and move toward resolving the issues.

1. Strive for Mutual Benefit. The ridiculousness of selfish, unsettled disputes was exhibited by a man in Cresco, Iowa a few years ago. He made a half-car garage out of a one-car garage by hiring a contractor to saw the structure in half. The sawing was the climax to a property-line dispute between Halsted and the owner of a small adjoining lot. When it was learned that Halsted's garage straddled the line between the two properties, negotiations over his use of the garage broke down, and he had the half not on his property cut down.

There is no use pursuing resolution to any conflict unless you are willing to seek an agreement that is mutually beneficial. It's imperative for people to focus on *what's* right for people, not *who's* right. I learned a long time ago that supposed winners in a conflict don't learn anything and losers never forget who stepped on them to get their way.

2. Seek Understanding. I am working on an invention that will revolutionize the world of negotiations. Once perfected, I predict this invention will eliminate conflict. What is it? An

Ego Enema. Countless relationship struggles would be solved if we could eliminate egos from the formula.

"If you don't agree with me," Sam Markewich said, "it means you haven't been listening." His comment would indicate that there are basically two sides to any argument—our side and the side that no intelligent, informed, breathing, sane, or self-respecting person could possibly hold. See what I mean about needing an Ego Enema?

Most people think they see the world as it is, but they don't. They see the world as they are. We perceive situations based on who we are, not on other people's perspectives. Try to see the world the way they see it. Be sensitive to others' emotions. Emotions are neither right nor wrong. Accept people and their opinions. Attempt to understand their perspective concerning the issues. Realize their priorities may not be yours, and the reasons behind their convictions could shed valuable light on the entire situation. Maintain calmness and patience as you listen to others talk. Accept your personal differences and move on.

3. *Focus on the Problem.* Get the facts. Don't rely on assumptions. Any time a conflict occurs, it is wise to make sure both parties are reading the same page. Refrain from attacking people and stay clear of arguing. Avoid fighting, battling, or

trying to overcome another's opinions or behavior. Insults, accusations, and blaming are dead-end strategies.

Aristotle had a good point. "How many a dispute could have been deflated into a single paragraph," he said, "if the disputants had dared to define their terms." Resolution isn't possible by dealing with symptoms. Define your terms by first defining the problem. Please make sure you agree on what the REAL problem is.

4. *Find a Point of Agreement.* You've heard it said that sometimes people just need to learn to agree to disagree. That might be true, but I much prefer a different approach before resigning myself to that conclusion. Cullen Hightower said: "There's too much said for the sake of argument and too little said for the sake of agreement." I like being around agreeable people with whom I can freely and openly discuss issues, concerns, or topics that we don't necessarily agree on. Being agreeable involves the ability to smile, nod, and express respect for another person's position.

Whenever you are intent on being disagreeable, other people will feel challenged and their intelligence will be questioned. Telling someone they are flat-out wrong will immediately raise the defenses, heighten their stubbornness, and cause them to be more adamant about their position.

How about agreeing to find out what we can agree on and committing our efforts to building on the things we can agree on and moving beyond the disagreements?

There is an old saying that goes, "Agree with thine adversary quickly." Help others be right about as many things as possible and you'll be amazed at how quickly the resistance will subside on other things.

5. *Generate Solutions.* Don't get stuck dwelling on the problem—just agree on it and then move on to the creatively stimulating process of generating solutions. "You cannot shake hands," said Golda Meir, "with a clenched fist." Neither can you generate solutions to a disagreement with a one-track mind or private agenda. What are ALL of the possible solutions that will produce a mutual benefit?

6. *Determine a Win–Win Plan of Action.* The motivation behind every conflict discussion should be to reach a point where we can genuinely agree on a solution that benefits each of us. Give way on the minor points of disagreement that have become a thorn in the flesh. Look for major points of agreement that will be mutually beneficial. Find ways to nurture the other person's self-esteem. Be likable, respectful, and considerate rather than being intimidating and demanding—you'll get much further. Try to love that person

There comes a time in the affairs of (people) when you must take the bull by the tail and face the situation.
W. C. FIELDS

on the other end as you accept differences and capitalize on agreements.

Too often people approach arguments like the man who said to his coworker: "OK, I'll meet you halfway. I will admit I'm right if you'll admit you're wrong."

In an issue of *Pulpit Helps* a humorous tale appeared about a hunter who had his gun aimed at a large bear and was ready to pull the trigger. Just then the bear spoke in a soft, soothing voice, saying, "Isn't it better to talk than to shoot? Why don't we negotiate the matter? What is it you want?" The hunter lowered his rifle and answered, "I would like a fur coat." "That's good," said the bear. "I think that's something we can talk about. All I want is a full stomach; maybe we can reach a compromise." So they sat down to talk it over. A little while later the bear walked away alone. The negotiations had been successful—the bear had a full stomach, and the hunter had a fur coat!

This far-fetched fable embodies healthy advice for arriving at win–win solutions (although had I been the hunter I believe I would have spent a bit more time in the generating-solutions stage). A great way to keep our horns unlocked is to start and end any discussion with these questions: "What is it the other person wants? How can both of our needs be met?"

WORK THROUGH IT

A husband and wife who were having problems in their marriage asked their pastor for counsel. After a rather lengthy session with them, he realized that he wasn't making any progress in resolving their conflicts. Noticing a cat and a dog lying side by side in front of the fireplace, he said, "Look at how peaceful they are. They certainly don't see eye to eye on everything." The husband commented, "Yes, but just tie them together and see what happens!"

Marriage is a mutual admiration society in which one person is always right, and the other is always the husband.

MARY MARTIN

"A marriage without conflicts," says Andre Maurois, "is almost as inconceivable as a nation without crises."

Maurois's comment reminded me of a judge in a divorce case who asked the husband, "Can you tell the court what passed between you and your wife during your heated argument that prompted the two of you to seek this separation?"

"I sure can, your honor," the man nervously responded, "there was a toaster, two knives, and a set of crystal."

Although amusing, this incident reminds us that conflict is normal; marital wars are dangerous.

Face it: The unique union of a man and woman is bound to create some issues of incompatibility. The transition from a casual to a formal relationship makes George Levinger's advice especially important. He said, "What counts in making a happy marriage is not so much how compatible you are, but how you deal with incompatibility. Differences that existed before marriage are intensified when we live with them. We come from different backgrounds, possess our own personality, see the world from unique perspectives, and are the unfortunate owners of irritating habits. We don't think alike, respond to life alike, or act alike. It can be frustrating. Rather than allowing the relationship to get tied up in knots, learn to loosen the noose a bit."

Author Charles Swindoll, writing in *Commitment: The Key to Marriage,* discusses the reality of conflict in marriage.

"There is no such thing as a home completely without conflicts. The last couple to live 'happily ever after' was Snow White and Prince Charming. Even though you are committed to your mate, there will still be times of tension, tears, struggle, disagreement, and impatience. Commitment doesn't erase our humanity! That's bad news, but it's realistic."

Although normal, work through conflict. Don't allow your behaviors to elevate it.

Ogden Nash suggested: "To keep your marriage brimming, with love in the loving cup, when you're wrong, admit it. When you're right, shut up."

There will always be a battle between the sexes because men and women want different things. Men want women and women want men.
GEORGE BURNS

A D I F F E R E N C E
O F O P I N I O N

In every house
of marriage
there is room
for an
interpreter.
STANLEY
KUNITZ

O

ur monthly card club tended to stray from the bridge game we came to play to conversations about local news, our children's activities, and sports events. One Saturday night a discussion ensued about marriage, men's irritating habits (from the women's perspective), and women's misconceptions about men (from the men's viewpoint). It was a lighthearted, give-and-take debate that digressed into a competition to see who could share the most cynical philosophy.

My favorite bantering came from a happily married couple with a great sense of humor.

The husband explained the key to their model marriage: "My wife and I understand each other. I don't try to run her life, and I don't try to run mine."

Not to be outdone, his wife responded, "The real secret to us staying married such a long time is simple, one of us talks, and the other doesn't listen."

AN IRISH PRAYER

May those who love us, love us;
And those who don't love us,
May God turn their hearts,
And if He doesn't turn their hearts,
May He turn their ankles,
So we'll know them by their limping.

GRATITUDE

Husbands, take your wife on at least one date a week. It doesn't have to be expensive (or fancy) but one that calls for dressing up a little for each other and providing undisturbed time together.

RALPH L. BYRON

KEEP THOSE FIRES BURNING

I t's no secret that romantic gratification or the lack of it are factors in every marriage. The idea of having one date together a week is a great way to keep the romantic fires burning. Undisturbed private time allows you to be continually reacquainted and in tune with each other's needs.

The following story provides a humorous look at one person's experience:

Mr. Smith came home from work early and found his wife in bed with a handsome young man. Just as Mr. Smith was about to storm out, she stopped him and said, "Before you leave, I'd like you to know how this happened.

"When I was driving home from shopping this afternoon, I hit a hole in the pavement. The hole was filled with water. Great blobs of mud spattered all over this man. Without a trace of anger, he looked at me and said, 'What rotten luck. I have a very important meeting this afternoon and just look at me!'

"I told him that I was terribly sorry and offered to clean him up. He seemed grateful, and I brought him home.

"He undressed in the bathroom, and I handed him the bathrobe I bought you for Christmas a few years ago. It no longer closes in front because of your pot belly.

"While his clothes were drying, I gave him lunch—the casserole you missed last night because you decided to go out with the guys after work. He said it was the best home-cooked meal he had had in months. I told him it was the first compliment I had received about my cooking in years.

"We talked while I pressed his shirt, and it was wonderful to have a conversation with a man who seemed interested in what I had to say. Suddenly he noticed the ironing board was wobbly. I had asked you a dozen times to fix it, but you were always too busy. The man fixed the ironing board in ten minutes, and then he actually put the tools away.

"As he was about to leave, he asked with a smile, 'Is there anything else your husband has neglected lately?' And that is the end of my story!"

James C. Dobson equals this story with one of his own. Dobson claims he knows an obstetrician who is deaf and blind in the same way. It seems the obstetrician called a physician friend of Dobson's, asking for a favor.

"My wife has been having some abdominal problems and she's in particular discomfort this afternoon," he said. "I don't want to treat my own wife and wonder if you'd see her for me?"

The physician invited the doctor to bring his wife for an examination, whereupon he discovered (are you ready for this?) that she was five months pregnant! Her obstetrician husband was so busy caring for other patients that he hadn't even noticed his wife's burgeoning pregnancy. "I must admit wondering," comments Dobson, "how in the world this woman ever got his attention long enough to conceive!"

James Smith wrote, "The tragedy of western marriages is that most of us quit courting once we're married."

Have you been taking your spouse for granted? What are you waiting for? Set the time now for your next date, and plan something unexpected to show your spouse that he or she is truly valued in your life.

The difference between courtship and marriage is the difference between the pictures in the seed catalog and what comes up.
AUTHOR UNKNOWN

HERE'S HOW TO PHRASE IT WHEN YOU WANT TO PRAISE IT

In spite of our supersonic generation, high-tech wizardry, and computer gadgetry, there is no technical tool equal to praise.
JERRY D. TWENTIER

U pon accepting an award, Jack Benny once remarked, "I really don't deserve this. But I have arthritis and I don't deserve that either."

Wouldn't it be great if appreciation would become as natural to give as undesirable life experiences were to contract? Yet how many times do small, seemingly insignificant actions go unnoticed? The doers of such tasks feel they would be better off getting attention in unacceptable ways.

Consider the employee who comes in late one morning only to be greeted by his supervisor who says, "Sam, you're late!"

Sam goes about his duties thinking, "So that's what I need to do to get noticed. Day in and day out I do my job without anyone paying any attention. Come in late and, finally, they know I'm working here."

People want to believe their efforts deserve praise, and they are willing to go to great lengths to receive it. Yet, expressing appreciation is one of the most neglected acts in relationships. When you observe people doing good things, let them know you recognized it. How? Glad you asked. Here are some simple phrases that will help you praise people and encourage them to repeat their positive behavior:

"I appreciate the way you . . ."

"I'm impressed with . . ."

"You're terrific because . . ."

"Thanks for going all out when you . . ."

"One of the things I enjoy most about you is . . ."

"I admire your . . ."

"Great job with . . ."

"I really enjoy working with you because . . ."

"Our team couldn't be successful without your . . ."

"Thank you for your . . ."

"You made my day when . . ."

"You can be proud of your . . ."

"You did an outstanding job of . . ."

"It's evident you have the ability to . . ."

"I like your . . ."

"You deserve a pat on the back for . . ."

"You should be proud of yourself for . . ."

"I admire the way you take the time to . . ."

"You're really good at . . ."

"You've got my support with . . ."

"What a great idea!"

"It's evident you have a special knack of . . ."

"You were a great help when . . ."

"You have a special gift for . . ."

"I enjoy being with you because you . . ."

"You're doing a top-notch job of . . ."

"It's fun watching you . . ."

"I know you can do it!"

"I believe in you."

"Your commitment to _____ is appreciated!"

The power of positive praise is limited only by its lack of use. How many people do you know who could benefit from a sincere "congratulations" or "great job" or possibly even "you're the best"? Silent appreciation doesn't mean much. Let others know you value them. They'll live up to your expectations.

Samuel Goldwyn said, "When someone does something good, applaud! You will make two people happy." I've provided a sampling of phrases you can use to applaud people. Use them frequently. Find additional ways to praise and increase people's good feelings about themselves. You'll be happy you did.

I believe that you should praise people whenever you can; it causes them to respond as a thirsty plant responds to water.
MARY KAY
ASH

VALUE YOUR FRIENDS

Friendship is a strong habitual inclination in two persons to promote the good and happiness of one another.

EUSTACE BUDGELL

Socrates once asked an elderly man what he was most thankful for. The man replied, "That being such as I am, I have had the friends I have had."

When we count up the truly valuable treasures of life, friendships certainly ought to be toward the top of the list. As all other tangible life rewards drift away, our friendships warrant whatever energy it takes to keep them alive and healthy. Consider the wisdom offered throughout history on ways to maintain, value, and enrich our friendships.

Friendship is built upon the commitment to be a friend, not upon the desire to have a friend.

AUTHOR UNKNOWN

If the people around you don't believe in you, if they don't encourage you, then you need to find some people who do.

JOHN MAXWELL

Do not use a hatchet to remove a fly from your friend's forehead.

CHINESE PROVERB

Any one who has had a long life of experience is worth listening to, worth emulating, and worth trying to have as a friend.

GEORGE MATTHEW ADAMS

The proper office of a friend is to side with you when you are in the wrong. Nearly anybody will side with you when you are right.

MARK TWAIN

A loyal friend laughs at your jokes when they're not so good, and sympathizes with your problems when they are not so bad.

ARNOLD H. GLASOW

The glory of friendship is not in the outstretched hand, nor the kindly smile, nor the joy of companionship; it is in the spiritual inspiration that comes to one when he discovers that someone else believes in him and is willing to trust him.

RALPH WALDO EMERSON

A true friend is one who hears and understands when you share your deepest feelings. He supports you when you are struggling; he corrects you, gently and with love, when you err; and he forgives you when you fail. A true friend prods you to personal growth, stretches you to your full potential. And most amazing of all, he celebrates your successes as if they were his own.

RICHARD EXLEY

Be careful the environment you choose for it will shape you; be careful the friends you choose for you will become like them.

W. CLEMENT STONE

Friend: One who knows all about you and loves you just the same.

ELBERT HUBBARD

You can always tell a real friend. When you've made a fool of yourself, he doesn't feel you've done a permanent job.

AUTHOR UNKNOWN

For further information about Glenn Van Ekeren's seminars and other products, contact:

Glenn Van Ekeren
1515 So. 175th Street
Omaha, Nebraska

Glenn Van Ekeren is Executive Vice President of Vetter Health Services. Previously he served as Director of People Development for Village Northwest Unlimited, an organization dedicated to meeting the needs of people with disabilities, and as President of People Building Institute, a seminar and consulting company committed to maximizing people and organizational potential. He shares his relationship principles with diverse audiences across the country as a frequent speaker and keynote presenter. He is the author of the *Speaker's Sourcebook* and *The Speaker's Sourcebook II*, and a featured author in several *Chicken Soup for the Soul* books.